ISABELLA ST.

TIRES

CAN
TIRE
TIRE COR

ISABELLA

DIAN TIRE CORPⁿ LIMITED
DIRECT FACTORY DISTRIBUTORS

CANADIAN
DIRECT FACTORY DISTRIBUTORS

TIRES

637

The
Longest Run
Your Money

Super-Lastic

CANADIAN TIRE CORPⁿ
LIMITED

SUPER LASTIC
MASTER
TRUCK TIRES

We Make Your
Dollars Go Further

RADIO
Tubes &
Supplies

BATTERIES

TIRES

The Longest Run for Your Money

OUR STORE

This book was made possible with the
generous assistance of:

W.B. DONER & COMPANY

QUEBECOR PRINTING CANADA

IBM

Solutions for a small planet™

Supported
by:

      CONSTRUCTION R. BRUNET (1987) INC.   Deloitte & Touche

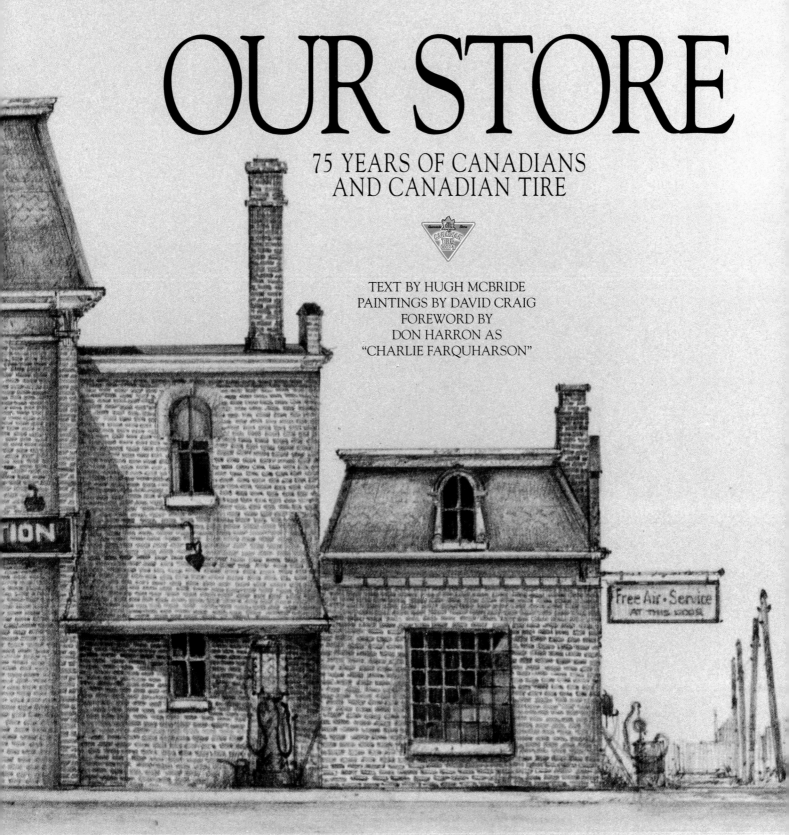

OUR STORE

75 YEARS OF CANADIANS AND CANADIAN TIRE

TEXT BY HUGH MCBRIDE
PAINTINGS BY DAVID CRAIG
FOREWORD BY
DON HARRON AS
"CHARLIE FARQUHARSON"

A QUANTUM BOOK PRODUCED FOR CANADIAN TIRE CORPORATION LIMITED

**Canadian Cataloguing in
Publication Data**

McBride, Hugh, 1957-
Our store: seventy-five years
of Canadian Tire and
Canadians

Produced for Canadian Tire
Corporation, Limited
ISBN 1-895892-10-4

1. Canadian Tire
Corporation - History.
I. Canadian Tire
Corporation. II. Title.

HD9745.C34C35 1997
338.7'6138112'097   C97-
931402-X

Produced by
Madison Press Books
for The Quantum
Book Group Inc.
149 Lowther Avenue,
Toronto, Ontario, Canada
M5R 3M5

Printed and bound in Canada

Contents

FOREWORD

PROLOGUE

CHAPTER ONE

Looking foreword to looking backerds at Canadian Tire

by Charlie Farquharson D.O.P.E. (Docterd of Personal Expeerients)

THE FURST THING I FOUND OUT ABOUT THIS bunch wuz that yer Canadian Tire is even oldern me. Charles Ewert Farquharson got bored in 1924, but them Tired peeples got berthed in 1922. I found this out wen I went to our lokel poast-offus fer a stamp and they sole me one with a pitcher on it of yer 2 founderers of this hole Tire organic-ization, yer Billes brothers.

Besides them 2 on that stamp is a foty-graft of a boy gittin' his furst bike frum his Dad, jist like wuz give to me by my old man back in 1939 wen the first

Canadian Tire deelership wuz open in Parry Sound by Cease McLean. (Our Cease had nuthin to do with eether the maggotzeen or yer tuth-paist of the saim naim.)

But I'm gittin offa the pint. I wuz so tickle I bot the hole book of them duzzen stamps celibating yer Canadian Tire 75th anaiversery. Mind, I pade the full price fer them guvmint stamps, with no mark-me-downs or disscounts. I shooda noan that yer Federasts isn't inta no bargins like yer Tire peeple all ways give me, pluss Canadian Tire munny so's I kin git to my rewards.

Wen I got back home frum the pust-offiss my male-box con-tane my 319 page Canadian Tire cattle-hog fer '97 with the Mable Leef stickin outa yer interminal Try-angel standin on its Ape-X. And the same yung lad and his bike and his Dad wuz also on the cuvver. We bin gittin them anual Tirebooks for dunky's yeers, but our dad wood never let us hang nun of them up in our

out-house, fer he clamed he needed to hole on to every page all yeer. Now we has us a indore skeptic tank and one of Canadian Tire's cushy skwishy paddied tilet seets.

Wen I wuz a yung tad us Farquharsons use to cum twice a yeer to the big sitty of Trauna. Once fer th'Ex, and the secund time fer yer Sandy Claws Prade. I wuz tookstrait to Canadian Tire fer to see Sandy McTire. He had even more of wat I wanted than that old Sane Nickle-us.

I mind the furst time I ever set fut in a Canadian Tire store wuz Labored Day of 1937 at ther mane flog-ship store on Yung Street hard by yer Davenport. All us Farquharsons (that's me 'n Mummindad, me bein

the only froot of ther loins) had cum all the ways down to the sitty of Trauma in Dad's bran new seckon handcar.

It wuz the time of yer Deep Depressyun, and Dad had gimme a quarter to spend on yer Canajun Nashnul Exhibitionists. ("Six bars a hat n'a bag all fer twenny fie sents!!" wuz wat they use to yell at the Poor Fud Bilding.) But Dad's furst stop wuz wat he deferred to back then as yer "Rub Her Tirin' Place." My muther wuz ankshuss to git on to the Flour Show, and I wanted to go on them Bumpy car rides on the Middleway, but

Dad sed furst things furst, and stopt us off at his faverit Tiring place.

Ackshully, lookin back on the hole thing, Mumm and I had more fun stairin at all the Canadian Tire stock between them iles than at yer so-call live stock at yer Exhibitionists. After all, we had all them animals of our own back home that wuz exhibit in yer Colossalino-leum. But in this big Tire store I had never seen such a Corny-copious of tools and artyfacks.

As a teeny-age boy standin in that store, I reelized that insted of becaming a farmer I wood mutch peefur to be one of them yung blades of sails-men on rollerskaits zippin' uppin down them Tire iles to the sound of Muzack. But like the old sayin' sez, the best plans of mice and men gits laid up pritty regler. In 1939, our guvmint had finely solve our unemployment problems by thinkin up World War Eleven, ware everybuddy wuz garnteed a job at a dollar thurty a day.

Us farmers wuz consider to be wat they called Ee-sensual Wore Wirkers, so we all got froze on our jobs. But in 1942 Ottawa brung in prescription fer our armed farces, so I jined me up in yer Royl Muskoka Dismounted Foot, and I wuz station hard by Barrie at yer Camp Boredom. I never got over-seized.

Nevertheless I got so blaim loanly stand-in on gard fer thee and me that I deranged to git engage to a low-cal Parry Sound girl, Valeda Drain, her being a Drain on her father's side and a Boyle on her muther's. I cooden afford a dymond ring at yer Burk's and ther wernt nuthin' sootabull at the navel store on our base, yer S.S. Kresge.

So I went over to yer Canadian Tirer in downtown Barrie fer to check the stock. In them daze, a lotta woretime things wuz bein rashind, like yer gas and yer rubbers goods. Despike that fack, I found me a nice cheep kitchin washer fer 49 sents that jist fit the Drain girl's finger. It did the job till Valeda and me got into holy acrimony in '45, wen I bot her a jin-a-wine Rindstone.

But I'm startin to digest agin. The eara of yer fifties wuz the start of yer Baby Bloomers wen everybuddy wanted a house fulla kids, wether they wuz ruriel, urbane or livin in yer sluburps. That's wen yer Canadian Tirers got morn more expansive. (Their bildins, not their prices!) Nowadaze they got deelers in yer Yewkon and yer NorthWasted TerrorTorys, so this big cumpny is bizzy doin deels frum mare to mare to mare. (Lattin fer "frum she to she to she" cuz morn thurty purrsent of their custom is frum wimmin.)

Us Farquharsons is jist hitch-hikers on yer inflammation hi-way, but weer determin not to be roadkill, and Canadian Tire keeps me in touch all the time with their freekwent flyers. They have aloud me to go on bein' self-defishunt, and to keep the promise I maid to myself wen I wuz a Boyscout with 3 fingers up: "Be Pre-paired!"

This here book makes me look backerds with nooralgia to my past yers, wile I'm still lookin forewerd to yer futures. (Bleeve me, on a farm yuh has to watch yer step in both places.) In all them 75 yeers that I bin bumpin my gums about, I keep thinkin of one time morn enny uthers. That wuz in 1940 wen we all had our backs up agin the wall during yer World War I Yi.

Wat cums to my mind is heerin' the vice over the raddio of that grate woretime Primer Minster Winsum Churchill. He wuz in the middel of yer Baddles frum Britten and inspyrin us all with his speaches, speshully wen he stole one of yer Canadian Tire slow-guns: "Give us the tools and we'll do the job arselfs!" ■

Our Store

A Saturday morning trip to Canadian Tire (above) is as much a part of a Canadian childhood as hockey practice or the first day of school. As adults we rely on the store for everything from maintaining the family car (opposite) to planning a camping trip.

ALONG WITH MAPLE SYRUP, MOUNTIES AND THE GREY CUP, Canadian Tire plays a part in defining us as Canadians. It's a role that extends far beyond next week's oil change or this week's special on power tools. Call it a feeling, a bond, a loyalty, call it whatever you want, but for hundreds of thousands of people there is something about their relationship with this particular store, with this store and no other. Transplanted to another country, would Canadian Tire be the same? Without it, Canada wouldn't be quite the same.

For many of us — especially those born after the Second World War — the relationship began with one of life's defining moments: say, the day our parents took us to buy our very first bicycle. In that instant, the store represented all the happiness and excitement we felt about our new possession, not to mention the freedom it made possible. In Canadian Tire, we came to see all that was shiny, new and wonderful — a glorious, bountiful pageant of affordable merchandise.

Of course there is more than sentiment to our allegiance. There's the simple, practical reality that Canadian Tire sells what we need and that there's a store within fifteen minutes travelling time of an astounding ninety percent of Canadian households. What's more, when shoppers arrive, they're confronted by a truly huge selection of competitively priced hardware, automotive parts and sports and leisure gear.

There's also something comfortable about the local Canadian Tire store — a comfort bred in part by familiarity, by knowing where everything is. There's no glitz or glamour, just honest, straight dealing, all very down-to-earth. There's more substance than show. It's comfortable, like an old pair of slippers.

And then there's Canadian Tire 'Money.' Something they give us when we pay in cash; something to reward us for choosing Canadian Tire. It's a voucher, really, nothing more. And look what's on it: that classic stereotype, Sandy McTire, everyone's idea of the penny-wise, canny Scotsman. But because it's printed on genuine bank-note paper, it feels real. And in a Canadian Tire store, it is.

More fundamentally, Canadian Tire has for seventy-five years helped us to recognize a quality that lies at the very heart of our national character: self-reliance. Many Canadians — Canadian Tire customers included — would rather pick poison ivy than pay someone to change the oil in their car or paint the bathroom. From the soapbox racers we built as kids out of boards and baby-carriage wheels, to the houses we maintain and improve as adults, Canadian Tire gives us the tools to do the job ourselves. And it is the place we associate with the deep satisfaction that comes from having done so.

The story of Canadian Tire is really many stories rolled into one. Principally, of course, it is the story of two men, cofounders J. W. and A. J. Billes, possibly at once the smartest and luckiest businessmen of their generation. They had the good fortune to enter the automotive-parts business at a time when the car was fast becoming accessible to all. But they leveraged that good fortune by shrewdly challenging established retail buying practices and thereby hitting on the perfect strategy for expansion. Their story is one of marketing genius, inspiration and hard, hard work.

Canadian Tire is also the story of stunning retail innovation in purchasing, marketing, information systems and, last but certainly not least, in the creation of a unique network of highly motivated, entrepreneurial Associate Dealers. Many of these individuals are tales in themselves. From humble beginnings, a number of them have risen to become leading business figures in the cities and towns they serve.

It's an impressive record of expansion. From one store in downtown Toronto in 1922, Canadian Tire grew to 116 locations by 1944, 171 by 1952, and 375 by 1983. Today, with 428 stores and 194 gas bars stretching from coast to coast, the company has sales of $3.91 billion.

The Canada-U.S. Free Trade Agreement, which took effect on January 1, 1989, brought about profound changes for Canadian businesses, including the country's established retailers. A number of American retailing behemoths entered the country, and many observers were prepared to write Canadian Tire's obituary. But as the 1990s unfolded, the Americans curtailed their expansion plans here. Canada, as it turned out, was no cakewalk. Meanwhile, despite the harsh business conditions, Canadian Tire remained profitable. Today, led by Stephen E. Bachand, a veteran of American do-it-yourself retailing, and a talented, outstanding management team, profits are up dramatically (more than $131 million in 1996) and the company is in the throes of expanding with new store layouts and computer systems, changes in product mix and greater efficiencies.

The history of Canadian Tire is, finally, the history of modern Canada. When the company was founded, Canadians were just becoming an urban people, and the car was only beginning to reshape our lives. Through the Depression and the Second World War, when the watchwords were *mend* and *make do*, the stores kept growing, helping customers to keep their cars running when they couldn't afford to buy new ones. Later, when Canada entered its long postwar boom, the stores followed them to the new suburbs, supplying the goods they needed to realize their dreams of affluence. As they have changed, it has changed. And today, Canadian Tire effectively represents its homeland — bilingual, urban and rural, stretching from sea to sea.

On this, the 75th anniversary of Canadian Tire's founding, there is much to celebrate.

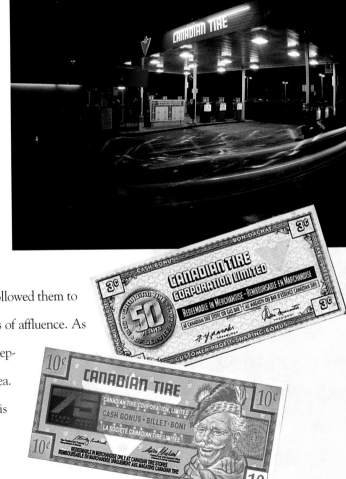

(Below) One of the 194 gas bars serving Canadians from coast to coast. The Canadian Tire guarantee (opposite) promises customers satisfaction with every purchase. Created as a promotional tool, Canadian Tire 'Money' (bottom and opposite) has become a national icon.

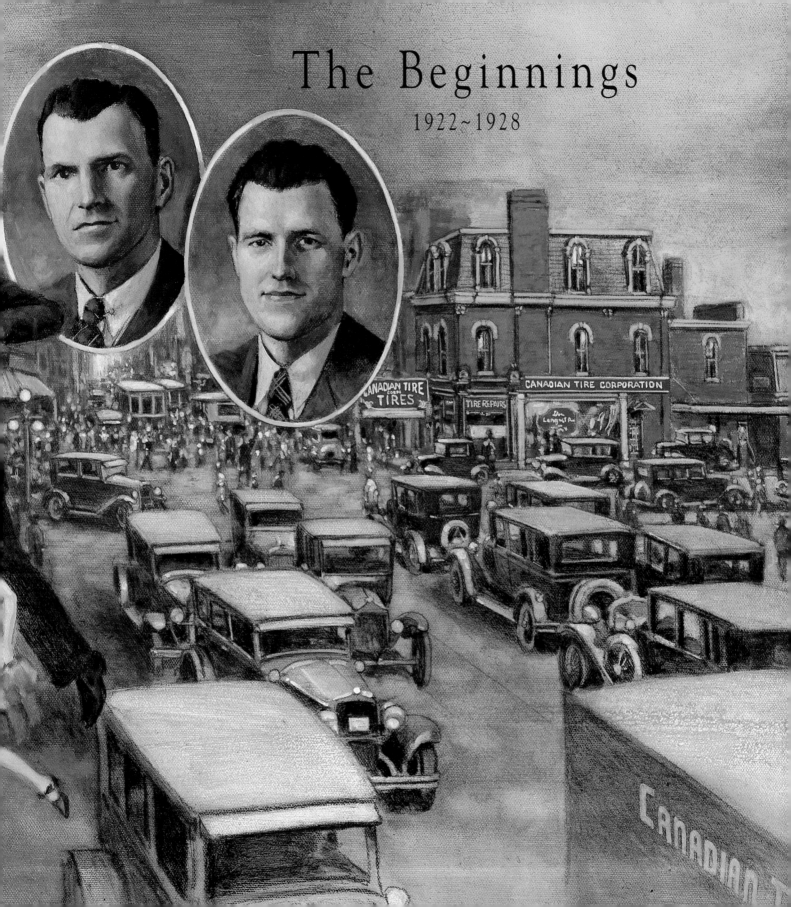

The Beginnings

1922~1928

The Beginnings

1922~1928

O
N THE MORNING OF SEPTEMBER 15, 1922, J.W. and A.J. Billes went to work, just as they had for the past nine years, to support their four sisters and widowed mother. But the situation on that early fall day, with the leaves on the trees just starting to turn, was distinctly different. The two brothers were going to work, not as employees, but as proprietors.

They had just purchased Hamilton Tire & Rubber, an automotive business located on the corner of Gerrard and Hamilton Streets in Riverdale, an east Toronto neighbourhood. For two young men starting out, money would have been a concern, so rather than taking a streetcar, they probably set out on foot from the family home, heading east.

The business was housed in a simple, nondescript two-storey brick building with a parking garage on the ground floor and a one-room office above. Across the street was Toronto's infamous Don Jail, a grim, imposing structure straight out of a Charles Dickens novel.

Although they did sell a few items, this was not a store — their business was parking cars. In those days, cars were a lot less reliable than they are now and notoriously difficult

Dapperly turned out in top hats and tails for a sister's wedding in the mid-twenties, the Billes brothers, John William and Alfred Jackson, share a joke.

to start, especially in cold weather. So if you had the money, as the doctors and lawyers living north of Gerrard did, you parked your car in a heated garage. Car theft was a serious problem — locks were unheard of — so the two brothers took turns sleeping overnight in the office to guard them. The Billeses were nothing if not mindful of the customer, and security was one service those paying to use the garage expected.

John William Billes, or Bill as he was called, was twenty-six at the time; his younger brother Alfred Jackson, or Alf, was just twenty. They were two of seven children, three boys, four girls, born to Henry and Julia Billes. Henry himself was among the youngest of twenty-two children born to Benjamin Billes, a prosperous soap maker in London, England. He grew up rich, but as the last among so many siblings, Henry saw little reason to wait around for his share of the family fortune. While in his early twenties, he left for Canada and settled in Toronto. There he met and married Julia Constable, daughter of a Toronto innkeeper.

Henry Billes became a butcher, eventually heading the shipping department at a wholesale meat company in Riverdale. Though not wealthy, the Billes family was comfortable.

Alf and Bill became business partners at an early age. Bill had a newspaper route and Alf helped out by sitting on the back of the wagon folding newspapers. Years later, A.J., as Alf was called for most of his life, recalled that when it was time to be paid, he would climb the stairs to the little-used second-floor bathroom at the family's home at 23 Sackville Street, which Bill called his "office," to receive his pay packet.

The burgeoning Billes family not long after the turn of the century.

From left, J.W., Julia Billes, A.J. (on Julia's lap), Evelyn, Averil, Henry Billes, Mae and Harry. Youngest of the clan, Elsie, had not yet been born when this photo was taken.

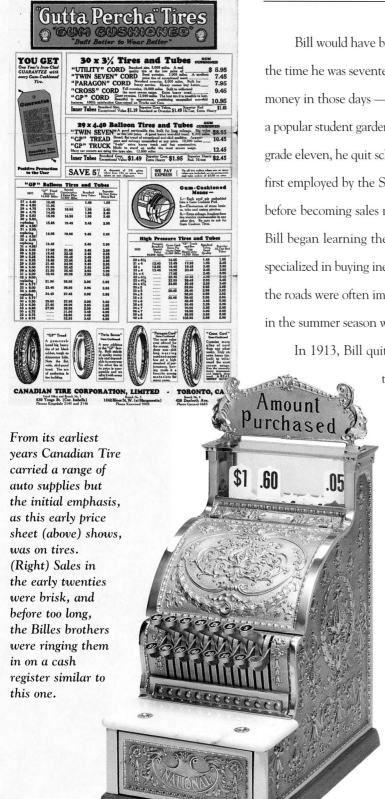

From its earliest years Canadian Tire carried a range of auto supplies but the initial emphasis, as this early price sheet (above) shows, was on tires. (Right) Sales in the early twenties were brisk, and before too long, the Billes brothers were ringing them in on a cash register similar to this one.

Bill would have been a superstar in any Junior Achievement program today. By the time he was seventeen, he had made one thousand dollars — a substantial sum of money in those days — by selling flower and vegetable seeds to the school board for a popular student gardening program. After finishing the third form, the equivalent of grade eleven, he quit school, where he studied accounting, and went to work. He was first employed by the Seeger Plumbing Company and Mack Truck as a bookkeeper, before becoming sales manager for Hamilton Tire & Rubber. While working there, Bill began learning the essentials of his future business. Hamilton Tire & Rubber specialized in buying inexpensive surplus tires from manufacturers in the winter, when the roads were often impassable and most cars were on blocks, and then selling them in the summer season when they were in demand.

In 1913, Bill quit his job and, in a fit of youthful exuberance, splurged on a trip to the west coast. The journey was out of character and he would never again indulge himself in quite the same way. While in Banff, Bill got word that his father had died of a heart attack while trying to break up a fight in the street between two men. Now the family's chief bread-winner, Bill returned to Toronto, penniless, to start supporting his mother and sisters. Alf, just twelve, quit school to do the same and found a job running errands for the Dominion Bank.

In 1922, the owners of Hamilton Tire & Rubber offered to sell the business to J.W., as Bill was now known, and A.J. for $1,800. Business that first year was poor. The Gerrard Street bridge across the Don River was closed for extensive repairs, turning the normally busy thoroughfare at their front door into a dead end.

Apart from the regulars, customers were scarce, and the brothers worked at other jobs to get by. In 1923, J.W. and A.J. closed the garage and briefly opened a retail outlet at Yonge and Gould Streets before settling in at Yonge and Isabella.

The new store carried a range of Ford and Chevrolet spare parts as well as batteries, toolboxes, radios, and an antifreeze that A.J. mixed in the basement. But tires were the Billes brothers' stock in trade. In those days, any of Toronto's forty thousand drivers were fortunate to make a trip to the country and back on a weekend outing without blowing a tire. In 1922, there were just one thousand miles of paved road in the whole country. Tires were flimsily

The Yonge and Isabella store as it appeared in 1925. Today, this building, with its distinctive mansard-style roof, still stands at the same intersection, though Canadian Tire's home office has moved farther north on Yonge Street.

J.W. brought his years of experience in the rubber business to the Billes brothers' new enterprise. At a time when car and truck tires were badly made and notoriously unreliable, he sought out products his customers could count on.

constructed and, by modern standards, wildly overinflated to fifty or sixty pounds of pressure. And they were expensive to replace. Indeed, they were one of the chief costs of car ownership.

If J.W. knew anything at this point, it was how to buy tires. "Having been connected with the rubber business, Bill knew of specials," A.J. told one journalist in the late 1980s. "We could usually buy seconds or some line that they wanted to get rid of. We were very, very fortunate — or maybe it wasn't just fortunate, because Bill really knew tires. And we never got stuck with a bad lot of tires."

By buying direct from factory jobbers and wholesalers, J.W. skipped the middleman's markup, and shaved the cost further by buying in bulk. In this way, the brothers handily undersold the competition. Not far down Yonge Street stood one of their main competitors, Consolidated Tire Stores, who billed themselves as the Largest Tire Dealers in Canada. In 1928, their lowest advertised prices didn't touch those of the Billes brothers.

There's no question that the brothers were in the right place at the right time. Once a luxury reserved for the rich, the car was becoming a means by which the common man could express his position, his prosperity and his individuality. It offered freedom to travel, to roam, to flee the familiar. As Heather Robertson put it in *Driving Force*, her study of GM Canada, "The driver was in control of a machine that magnified human speed and power to a degree that no one had ever before experienced."

In 1911, there were just twenty thousand registered vehicles in the entire country. By 1920, the number had risen meteorically to four hundred thousand and by 1930, there were fully one million drivers on the roads, eighty thousand miles of which were now paved, thanks to a massive road-improvement drive in the 1920s.

Right from the start, the Billes brothers distinguished themselves with their catalogue copy. Who could resist a purchase that included "All taxes paid," "Free delivery," "Free service" and was topped off by a written guarantee?

21

Owning a Car in the Twenties

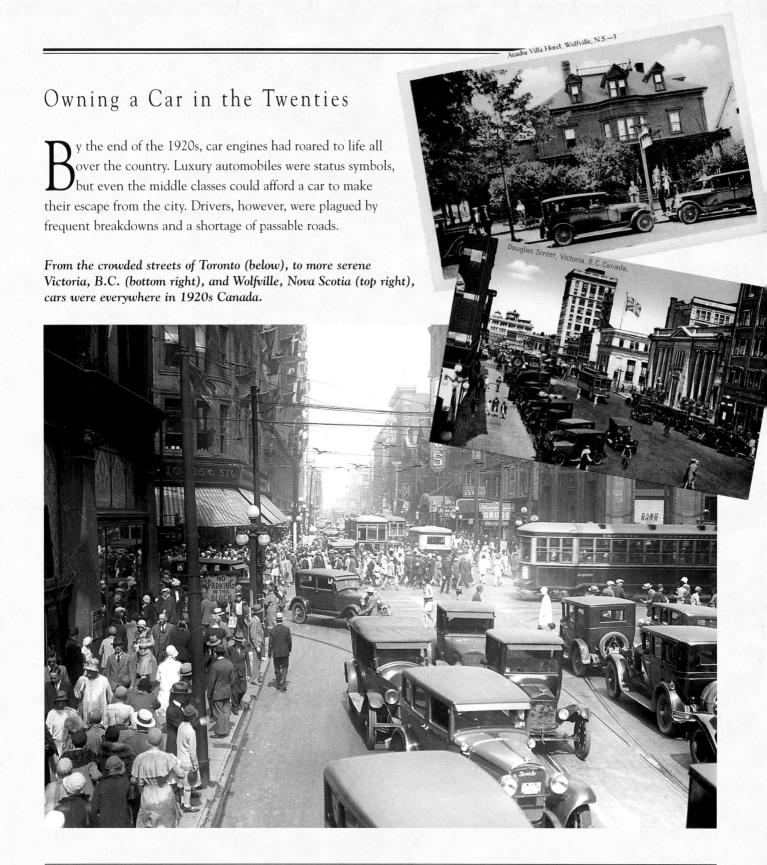

By the end of the 1920s, car engines had roared to life all over the country. Luxury automobiles were status symbols, but even the middle classes could afford a car to make their escape from the city. Drivers, however, were plagued by frequent breakdowns and a shortage of passable roads.

From the crowded streets of Toronto (below), to more serene Victoria, B.C. (bottom right), and Wolfville, Nova Scotia (top right), cars were everywhere in 1920s Canada.

Acadia Villa Hotel, Wolfville, N.S.—3

Douglas Street, Victoria, B. C. Canada.

Though 1920s advertisements promised that the automobile would bring luxury and ease (above and below), car owners of this era were more often found scrubbing the car in the river (top left), circling for a parking space (middle left), or soiling a shirt while changing a tire (bottom left).

The straight-eight is the ultimate motor principle. Hupmobile is its finest expression. The combination means that there literally is nothing more distinguished in motoring

Beauty, Color Options, Luxury in ten enclosed and open bodies

IN THE FINE CAR FIELD, THE TREND IS UNDOUBTEDLY TOWARD EIGHTS

THE DISTINGUISHED HUPMOBILE EIGHT

The Billeses made it their business to see that car ownership was, if nothing else, affordable. This was the basic ingredient in their success, and they never wavered.

The brothers soon introduced an unconditional guarantee on every tire sold. "In those days the guarantee on tires was only for defects and workmanship," A.J. recalled. "A customer would come in with a shard of glass or a stone bruise, saying, 'Well, I didn't do that,' so I introduced the first guarantee. People came in looking for a fight, and there wasn't one."

This policy brought in scores of new customers, and by 1925 the brothers had moved to a larger location at 639 Yonge Street. Customer interest was so great that, as a result of advertisements in the *Toronto Star*, inquiries came pouring in from well beyond the city. Soon, the Billeses had a burgeoning mail-order business. To reflect the growing scope and potential of the operation, the brothers chose to incorporate as Canadian Tire Corporation. "We used Canadian Tire because it sounded big," A.J. said.

Astute purchasing was only one half of the Billes brothers' formula for success. They were clever marketers as well. "Super-Lastic" was the name they chose for their tires and it was written prominently on the Yonge Street store. Emblazoned nearby was the slogan, The Longest Run for Your Money, illustrated by a smiling tire running along as fast as his super-lastic legs could carry him.

"Gum Cushioned Tires ... The World's Best ... Save 5¢ Per Gallon ... Gas at Cost!" announced a Canadian Tire newspaper advertisement in 1928. "Buy a tire and tube, get 5¢ off your gas for the year. Why? To show you our appreciation of your tire business in a real, tangible way, and to fully bear out our slogan: We Make Your Dollars Go Farther."

To cater to its growing mail-order business, Canadian Tire put out its first price sheets in 1926. On one side were road maps of Ontario and the Maritimes, where the company was also doing more and more business. At a time when maps were hard to come by, this approach virtually guaranteed that the price sheets would be seen and used. The first Canadian Tire catalogue, still with road map, followed in 1928.

Key to the Billes brothers' success was their understanding of the power of marketing. Catchy slogans (below), special offers and an unconditional guarantee on every tire sold distinguished Canadian Tire from its competition. One of the attractions of Canadian Tire's early price sheets (opposite) was the useful road map printed on one side.

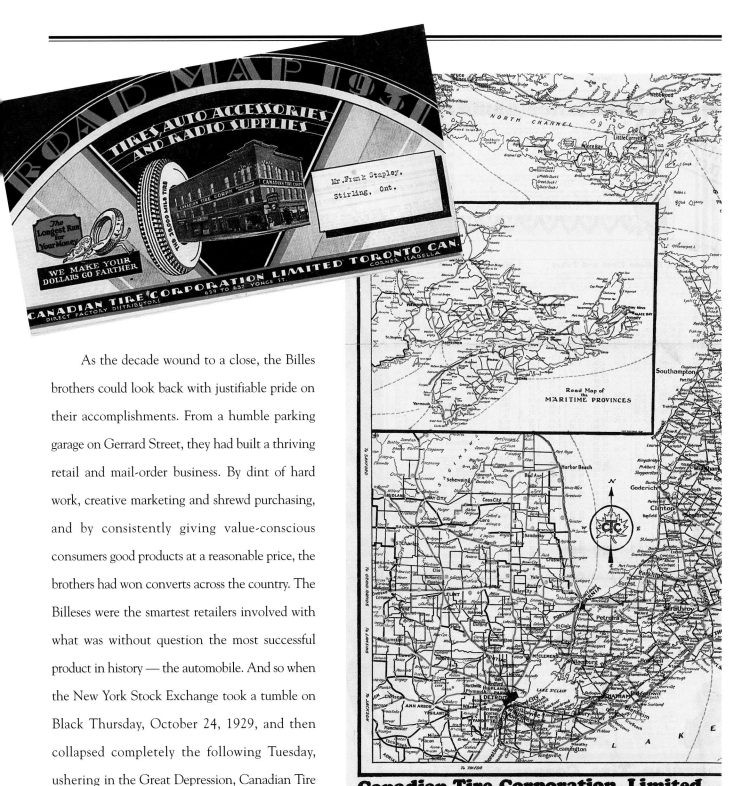

As the decade wound to a close, the Billes brothers could look back with justifiable pride on their accomplishments. From a humble parking garage on Gerrard Street, they had built a thriving retail and mail-order business. By dint of hard work, creative marketing and shrewd purchasing, and by consistently giving value-conscious consumers good products at a reasonable price, the brothers had won converts across the country. The Billeses were the smartest retailers involved with what was without question the most successful product in history — the automobile. And so when the New York Stock Exchange took a tumble on Black Thursday, October 24, 1929, and then collapsed completely the following Tuesday, ushering in the Great Depression, Canadian Tire looked like a good bet for riding out the storm.

Canadian Tire Corporation, Limited
629-637 Yonge Street [Cor. Isabella Street] Toronto, Can.

It Happened in the Twenties

THE DECADE THAT WITNESSED THE BIRTH OF CANADIAN TIRE Corporation was one of deep and profound change in every aspect of Canadian life. The nation emerged from the end of the Great War in 1918 flush with self-confidence and renewed nationalism. And why not? Canada had succeeded in waging the largest military campaign in its history — by far. Canadian soldiers proved themselves the equal of any Allied or German soldier. "Whenever the Germans found the Canadian corps coming into line," British Prime Minister David Lloyd George observed at the time, "they prepared for the worst."

The war had been costly — more than sixty thousand lives had been lost — and the federal government was deep in debt, the result of

The Union Jack on the Red Ensign and the lyrics of "The Maple Leaf Forever" in the postcard pictured above emphasize the close ties the Dominion still enjoyed with Britain throughout this decade. (Below) Edward, Prince of Wales, visits the 1927 Canadian National Exhibition for a celebration of the Diamond Jubilee of Confederation. (Right) The Edmonton Grads, Canada's celebrated women's basketball team, who under coach Percy Payne (centre) dominated the sport for more than two decades, were declared world champions in 1924.

the huge capital outlay needed to train, equip and send four hundred thousand troops overseas. Canada's debt stood at $3.5 billion, seven times the prewar level. Credit was tight. Taxes were raised. And not until the latter half of the decade did Canadians — those outside the Maritimes, that is — come to enjoy prosperity and economic growth. In Canada, the 1920s were not roaring.

Times were difficult as the widespread labour unrest of 1919 indicated, but the war had helped modernize the Canadian economy. Importation of British goods was neither practical nor reliable during wartime, so Canadian producers moved to fill the vacuum. The range of products made in Canada grew accordingly. Even as individual Canadians were paying the ultimate price in defence of Britain, economic ties between the two countries were weakening. Canada was becoming more self-reliant. Political independence followed on increasing economic independence: by 1931, the Statute of Westminster would make Canada fully self-governing.

A still from *Sergeant Cameron of the Mounted, a Hollywood fantasy of life in the Canadian Rockies.*

Also during the twenties:

• Manufacturing and resource industries such as mining and pulp and paper grew more important, and cities proved the major beneficiaries. In 1921, for the first time in the nation's history, there were more urban than rural Canadians.

• In arts and entertainment, Stephen Leacock emerged as Canada's greatest humourist. Seven artists who painted the Canadian landscape formed the Group of Seven. The country's first commercial radio station began broadcasting in Montreal in 1921, and the Talkies, movies with sound, were thrilling audiences by 1927.

• Canadian inventions during the 1920s included Pablum, the snowmobile and quick-frozen food. Most significant of all was the discovery of insulin, which would increase the quantity and quality of life for diabetics around the world.

• In sports, the Ottawa Senators won the Stanley Cup four times, in 1920, 1921, 1923 and 1927.

• The country's first social-security measure was enacted in the form of a meagre old-age pension.

Hard Years

1929-1945

CHAPTER TWO

Hard Years

1929~1945

FOR MILLIONS OF CANADIANS, THE GREAT DEPRESSION MEANT HUNGER, POVERTY and destitution. The old newspaper and magazine photographs tell the horrifying story: images of drought-stricken Prairie farmland devastated by dust storms, of rural families evicted by mortgage companies, of tin-and-tarpaper shanty towns and soup-kitchen line-ups. Between 1928 and 1933, Canadians' income fell on average by almost fifty percent. By 1933, close to one million people were without jobs; this out of a population of just eleven million and at a time when there wasn't any unemployment insurance, organized welfare system, or social safety net.

And yet, through it all, cars and trucks rolled inexorably forward. If people couldn't afford a new car, then they still needed gas and parts for the old one. And in such a climate Canadian Tire, the Billeses and their employees not only prevailed, but flourished. Businesses everywhere were closing their doors. But not Canadian Tire.

By the early 1930s, amid the service bays, sales counters and offices at Yonge and Isabella streets, a durable and distinctive corporate culture, inspired by the two men in charge, was quietly taking shape.

Together, J.W. and A.J. Billes formed the perfect management team. J.W. handled purchasing and administration; A.J., the sales, mail order and service departments.

As president, J.W. provided the sense of direction and the firm, guiding hand. Stolid, reserved, cautious, distant, he was the solitary captain whose eyes seemed never to waver,

A Depression-era road map features the Billes brothers, their staff and the assurance that the store is "100% Canadian in personnel and product."

who focussed intently on a distant horizon that no one else could see quite as clearly. A.J., as vice-president, was his opposite: a gregarious, collegial, energetic risk taker. He helped his staff with the most menial of tasks. His energy and enthusiasm knew no bounds, rubbing off on everyone around him.

"Alf was a motivator in many ways," veteran employee Mayne Plowman recalls. One day, just before closing time, A.J. sold a fellow a set of four tires. "Okay, Mayne," he said, "I've got four tires to go on here. You take one side and I'll take the other and we'll see who beats."

The work week had six days, and those days were long and hard. You worked from 8:30 A.M. until 10 P.M. for three days and from 8:30 A.M. until 6:00 P.M. the rest of the week. But everyone knew that if you did your job well you would be rewarded — handsomely.

Myrel Pardoe found this out right away. In April 1932, when she was just sixteen years old, she took her very first job, opening the mail at Canadian Tire for eight dollars a week. Her work must have been good. When they gave out the semi-annual bonuses that June, just two months after she started, she got a six dollar cheque — almost a week's wages! And that December she received thirty-five dollars.

"I was *so* proud," she says in a sweet lilting voice, sixty-five years later.

Myrel Pardoe still works for Canadian Tire. She's the longest-serving employee in the Corporation, has been for twenty years. When she started, there were just twelve employees.

Myrel Pardoe (above) has worked for Canadian Tire since 1932. Here she is shown in 1952 on her 20th anniversary. (Below) In the early 1930s Canadian Tire promised their customers delivery of out-of-stock items within an hour. This truck (right) helped them keep that promise.

Owning a Car in the Thirties

A Sunday drive on one of Canada's inadequate roads in the 1930s could end in muddy disaster (*above*). Here a team of horses is required to assist. Despite the Depression, there were still those who could afford vacations (*right*) and new cars (*below left*). For those who could not, the "Drive-it-Yourself" ride at Hanlan's Point on Toronto Island (*below right*) offered drivers of all ages the pleasures of motoring without the responsibilities.

THE WASAGA INN—WASAGA BEACH—CANADA

The dream of a national radio service first saw light as the Canadian Radio Broadcasting Commission in 1933. But it really got going with the founding of the CBC in 1936. For those contemplating buying a radio from the 1937 catalogue (which helpfully suggested that cash was the best form of payment), one sure treat would be listening to the wacky songs and comedy of the Happy Gang, which started its twenty-two year run that summer.

Supertone RADIOS

BUY FOR CASH AND SAVE

We buy for Cash! . . . in large quantities . . . direct from the manufacturers. We offer them to you . . . also for cash . . . but at substantial discounts. We have no 'credit losses or costly re-possessions . . . we need only a small profit.

Supertone
BATTERY RADIOS

Including Batteries and Tubes

Style A—As illustrated. A fine modernistic mantel 4 tube set with 6 tube functions. Full vision dial and numerous features. A most outstanding buy at this low price **$34.95**

Style AA—Same chassis as Style A but with larger speaker and mounted in full size console cabinet of outstanding beauty **$46.95**

***Style "B"**—6 tube All-Wave Mantel set with every worth-while, up-to-the-minute feature. A new speaker of revolutionary design, puts this set in a class by itself **$52.95**

***Style CD**—5 tube All-Wave Console model (see cabinet marked "D"). This is a fine set of outstanding beauty and with many unique engineering features **$59.95**

[...] tube All-Wave full size [...] embodying same speaker [...] out 10" in diameter. [...] more enjoyably heard [...] your own home will [...] at there is nothing [...] of **$69.95**

[...] marked, may be purchased [...] xtra cost of $7.00, [...] r unit which eliminates [...] dry "B" Batteries. [...] ate on any 6 volt [...] attery of your own [...] ets so equipped do [...] tery and we refer [...] ices.

CAMERON [...] ANTENNA

[...] most efficient, [...] asily installed [...] erial system [...] ilt by "Trico". [...] mes complete [...] h Litz wire, [...] ll hardware and complete [...] instructions for mounting. This outfit is listed at $5.00. Our price is listed **$1.89**

STYLE "A"

STYLE "D"

Supertone
A.C. ELECTRIC SETS

Style "C". Console model, All-Wave, similar to above but with larger, finer speaker giving richer tones and great fidelity. Cabinet similar to "D" but measures 40" high, 23" wide **$54.95**

Style "D". 7 tube Chassis having 9 tube functions. An entirely new system of audio amplification has been built into this receiver resulting in tone qualities far above anything heretofore produced. All-Wave of course with complete tuning range—electron ray tuning indicator as well as all the other worth while new features. Compare this set with anything available regardless of price and you'll be convinced we have the radio buy of the year **$69.75**

ALL-WAVE AERIAL

All-Wave Radios will not operate to any degree of satisfaction with an ordinary aerial. After a great deal of thought and experiment this system has been perfected to fill every requirement for any make of radio. All parts are of the highest quality and kit comes complete with full instructions.

Kit consists of 100 ft. 5 strand aerial wire, 50 ft. (pair) weather-proof transmission line, Short Wave antenna coupler, 1 porcelain junction block, 4 glass insulators, 2- 6" bakelite screw eyes, double lightning arrester, double window lead-in strap, Shur-grip Ground Clamp **$2.98**

MASTER AERIAL KITS $1.39

Improve reception by replacing that weather-beaten aerial. Our kit includes lightning arrester, 75-foot heavy 7 x 22 copper aerial wire. 40-foot lead-in wire, ground strap, window lead-in strap, insulators, screw eyes, etc.

The HAPPY GANG

EDDIE ALLEN   GEORGE TEMPLE   BLAIN MATHE   BERT PEARL   KAY STOKES   BOB FARNON   HUGH BARTLETT

Today, Canadian Tire Corporation, Limited and its Associate Dealers can boast of some thirty-four thousand.

Ask Myrel why she's stayed with Canadian Tire for so long and you'll find in her answer a clue to the loyalty the Billeses commanded, the corporate culture they fostered and the work ethic of another time and place.

"In those days we took *pride* in what we were doing," she says haltingly, deliberately. "And we *cared* about the company ... we *cared* about people.... Somebody asked us to do something, and we did our *utmost* to do what they wanted. You never questioned things the way young people do today."

It was all very simple, really. You were grateful to have a job because jobs were hard to come by. You showed your gratitude by being loyal, dedicated and hardworking. "There just weren't jobs," she says emphatically. "People had no money. And so if you got a job you stayed at it." Myrel Pardoe is still doing just that.

This sort of dedication made Canadian Tire flourish. In the 1934 catalogue, Canadian Tire was described as "The Largest Direct Automotive Supply House in Canada" — *direct* meaning no middlemen, no unnecessary markups, and products at the best possible price. In fact, Canadian Tire didn't have any competition in the mail-order business. Sure, Eaton's and Simpson's sold a lot of merchandise by catalogue. But their automotive product lines were no match for the Billeses'. Inside the twenty-four-page spring edition, still featuring a road map on the cover as an attractive bonus, was a bevy of products just right for the cash-strapped thirties' customer. House paints were listed at $2.98 a gallon; "baby auto hammocks" at $1.89 and tire covers at $0.89. A top recover for a 1928 Chev went for just $5.95.

Many of the pages were filled with the kind of car accessories that, thankfully, are standard equipment today: heaters, and manual and automatic "windshield cleaners"(that's what wipers were called back then), not to mention auto trunks (deluxe, large-size for $18.65). Elsewhere in the catalogue there were accessories we can barely envision today, including window "anti-rattlers" costing twenty-two cents and, at twelve cents each, pneumatic

In the spirit of mend and make-do, handy car owners of the thirties and forties could purchase "Auto Tops" and other car accessories, as this 1943 catalogue page demonstrates.

House brand products from the 1930s and 40s, like the spark plugs (above) and glass cleaner (below), focussed attention on the value and quality Canadian Tire had to offer.

cushions designed to silence those pesky loose car doors. J.W.'s catalogue copy was crisp, precise and fun to read, with a sales pitch that was hard to resist. The writing carried you forward, like a car that had popped its clutch. "Use Canadianize Wax and Cleaner," he exhorted. "You've tried the others ... now try the best. A faster and more thorough cleaner — a harder and more durable wax."

As young retailers a decade before, J.W. and A.J. quickly grasped the importance of house brands. The Super-Lastic brand launched in the 1920s gave them the flexibility to switch to the lowest-price brand of tires available. Private brands were also good advertising — they sold the virtues and benefits of the product while imbuing them with credibility. Now the Billeses added Mor Power Super Bilt batteries, Moto-Master Super Bilt spark plugs, Moto-Master oil and Master Mixed paint and varnish. Super-Cycle bicycles and MasterCraft power tools would come later.

In 1936, J.W. decided to expand the company's product line. In so doing, he laid the foundation for Canadian Tire's huge popularity in the years to come. Back then, as today, the most frequent driving was back and forth to work. Even so, drivers preferred to see their cars in a more romantic light, to think of them in terms of freedom. They provided a chance to flee a cramped and crowded urban existence for, say, a picnic in the country. So, J.W. ruled, the store selling you products for your car would also sell you the tents, camping stoves, golf clubs and other sporting goods you would need when you arrived at your idyllic destination.

The spring 1936 edition of the catalogue was one great proclamation of leisure-time possibilities. The cover featured an illustrated woodland paradise. Mom cheerfully worked the camping stove. Dad fiddled with a fishing rod, and out on the lake, some lucky fellow steered his motorboat into a glorious sunset. In the foreground stood the car that got them there.

The year 1936 saw another profound change. In 1930, pressed for space, the company moved one door south, to 625-637 Yonge. This site, some thirty-five thousand square feet spread over three floors, seemed so large — so dauntingly, dangerously (in terms of financial risk) large — that the brothers sublet part of it. But business was going so well in the early thirties

The Great Outdoors

In the late 1930s, Canadian Tire started carving out a bigger role for itself in the leisure time of Canadians. Whether one was on a fishing trip in Ontario (*above left*) or a hunting expedition in Nova Scotia (*above right*), Canadian Tire wanted their customers to know that they could supply the needed goods (*right and below*).

ON OUT-OF-TOWN ORDERS   101

"The Canadian" MOTORIST TENTS $26⁹⁵

Complete
9'x9'
7' high
No. S700

The popular style for the tourist and motor camper. Can be erected speedily and easily by one person. Storm tight. Water-proofed **Buff Canatite**. **"Sewn-in" Water** proof Floor. **Screened Window** in the rear with storm flap adjustable from the inside. **Mosquito Door Screen**. **Awning Extension** full width of the eaves, as well as a **Roll Flap Storm Door**. Supplied complete with jointed awning poes and centre pole, pegs; four iron eave rods with elbows, and bag for tent.

MASTER
SLEEPING
BAG

**Eiderdown
Filled**
33" x 72"

Down liner is constructed from down-proof sail silk and stitched to keep the filling evenly arranged and is filled with warm doeskin and storm collar is strong warm doeskin ... cover. Slide fastener down one ... comforter on a bed

CANADIAN TIRE CORPORATION LIMITED *Spring and Summer* 1941

NAME THE COVER CONTEST SEE PAGE 4

(Right) "Tackle 'em right and they're sure to bite," boasted this fishing spread in the 1940 catalogue. The wilderness expedition symbolizes Canadian life in the period postcard at top. To help with the legendary "one that got away" (above), Canadian Tire offered "real reel values" (opposite).

Tackle

"Good Rods at a Better Price"

No. S414. A fine **3-piece tubular steel casting rod.** Offset handle, cork grips, agatine guides, attractively wound with bright alloy wire on a ...an rod with black trim. **$2.25** 4½' or 5' ....

No. S415. Special analysis alloy steel **1-piece** squared tip with built-in action. Beautiful brown tone finish, agatine guides and hardened steel tip-top chrome plated. New tri-lock handle locks both rod and reel securely together. **$4.35** 4½' or 5' ....

No. S416. Get pleasurable casting with this non-twisting flat **"Nu-Grip Actionized"** rod. Has vacuum-fit forward grip on a silver finished hexagon shaped special analysis alloy steel tip. Red agatine guides and hardened steel tiptop. Red and black trim. A delightful rod. 4½' or 5' **$5.25**

No. S411. **Telescopic bait rod** extends to 8½'. Reversible handle with solid cork grip, nickel plated reel seat, agatine guides and tip. Three joints **$1.95**

No. S413. Same as No. S411 but has four joints **$2.25**

No. S412. A **4-joint telescopic casting rod** with detachable double cork grip handle with finger hook. Agatine guides and top on nickel silver bands. Length 5' **$2.79**

No. S409. A 4 ft. heavy duty **Trolling Rod** with double corrugated wood grips and rubber butt cap. Graduated blade with just the right flexibility. Nickel silver guides and agatine tip top **$1.39**

No. S415 · No. S416 · No. S409 · No. S417 · No. S413 · No. S404 · No. S414 · No. S400

"True Temper Made" Special Most outstanding value in a quality rod at a popular price. **"Squared"** tapered alloy steel **chrome plated** tip, with agatine guides and tip. Full size double cork grip on an offset aluminum handle. 4½'. No. S400. Only **$2.45**

"Master Cast" Special A well balanced **cadmium** finished **squared** tapered tip, attractively trimmed with red. Aluminum offset handle with **screw-lock reel seat.** Agatine guides and special hardened **steel tip top.** 4½'. **No. S417.** Only **$1.98**

REAL REEL VALUES

No. S310. "Shakespeare Criterion De Luxe." This beautiful model is a classic reel creation . . . the perfect reel. Diamond hard-chrome over nickeled brass frame, stainless steel bushings, patented instant takedown level wind. Split cork arbor furnished. Thumb operated click and adjustable drag **$6.95**

No. S311. "Shakespeare New Criterion." A radiant beauty with embossed headplate, and exceptionally smooth running spool, jewelled spool caps, quiet spiral gears, adjustable compensating brake. Level wind of course **$5.75**

No. S308. "Shakespeare Triumph." A 3-unit brass reel, circle chrome finish, phosphor bronze bushings, unusually silent hard steel and brass gears. thumb operated click, adjustable tail drag, adjustable crystal agate spool caps, take-down level wind. Approx. 100 yd. capacity **$4.85**

No. S319. "Shakespeare New Imperial." Bright nickel chrome on brass, phosphor bronze steel bearings, jewelled spool caps, with click, and hard chrome plate level wind. Capacity about 125 yds. **$3.75**

No. S302. A beautiful all brass quadruple multiplying reel, heavily chrome plated. Tenite handle knobs, jewelled end caps. Level winding, scientifically built for speedy free action. Attractive embossed design on end plate. Unusual at **$2.49**

No. S304. A sturdy reel of heavily chromium plated steel. Jewelled spindle caps are adjustable. End plates are beautifully engraved. Adjustable click. Tenite handle knobs. Only **$1.79**

No. S300. Level wind of serviceable construction, and good to look at. End plates and bearings of time tested "Permo." Smooth live action. Capacity 80 yds. Special **$1.09**

No. S311 · No. S308 · No. S319 · No. S302 · No. S300

No. S401. A **"True Temper"** made "hit." A solid steel **casting rod.** Gun metal enamel finish with cream colored sheath and trim. Wire wound garnix mountings, offset handle, double cork grips. 4½' or 5' **$3.59**

No. S403. **"True Temper Challenge"** rod with a cadmium plated tempered steel tip, 4'3" long overall. Double cork grip on offset polished aluminum handle. Garnix guides and stainless steel tip top. Correct flexing and balance **$4.19**

No. S404. **"True Temper Oxford."** A beautiful cadmium plated custom-made type rod. Square forged, tapered, heat treated selected steel tips with agatine guides. Black polished reel seat on the famous Speedlock handle. Cork main grip and black Tenite forward grip. 4½ ft. It's got "IT" **$7.45**

No. S406. **"True Temper Oxford."** Seamless tubular steel tip. By a patented and exclusive process the tubes are drawn to a taper providing marvellous controlled flexibility. Agatine guides. Offset aluminum handle with burnished reel seat and double cork grips. 5 ft. **$7.25**

No. S314. "Shakespeare New Classic." A handsome feather-light level-winding reel that will stand the severest test of the hardest practical fishing. Flint hard finish, new adjustable gear shell drag, operated by a knurled thumb wheel. A superb model **$7.50**

No. S301. Trolling Reel. A 250 yard free spool lever sturdy reel with black bakelite ends. Has left end bearing cap, spiral gears, and back sliding click **$2.29**

No. S301 · No. S305

THUMBLESS "WONDEREEL"

No. S305. You don't need a thumb with Shakespear's new Thumbless "Wondereel." Anyone, regardless of previous fishing experience can cast the average ⅝ oz. lure with little effort and, **without fear of backlash.** Popular 3-piece design, with oversize tail bearing, adjustable head end spool cap, aluminum spool and crank. Shakespeare Quality at **$7.50**

that in no time, space was once again at a premium and the sublet area was reclaimed. In the cramped confines of the service department, for example, moving cars around had become a real problem. Sometimes, to move one car in or out, several others had to be jockeyed as well. The solution was a turntable, not unlike those used in railway roundhouses, that ran on eight-inch steel wheels and a circular track embedded in the floor.

By the mid-1930s the store was causing havoc in the neighbourhood. "The people on Isabella Street were continually complaining, and with every right," the late Norm Jones, an early employee, recalled. "It was almost impossible for them to get along the street to their homes because of the many transport and freight trucks parked on the sidewalks.... Customers' cars were parked all over the place, waiting to get into the service department." Relief was on the way.

In 1935, a few blocks north on Yonge Street, government officials had proudly unveiled the new Grand Central Market, an uptown version of Toronto's venerable St. Lawrence Market. With its arched facade and terrazzo

By 1936 the Billes brothers were ready to move uptown to a larger and grander location at Yonge and Davenport (above). So massive was this new building (right and below) that many wondered if all the space would ever be filled.

floors, the sprawling two-storey structure seemed to hold court at the busy intersection of Yonge and Davenport. Within a year, however, the food stalls and fresh produce were gone. A new market in the Dirty Thirties proved a dismal failure. J.W. snapped the place up.

In the fall of 1936, as employees moved merchandise and equipment to the new store, many wondered what in heaven's name they would do with all the space. The store was 212 feet from front to back. "This is one hell of a big building," Canadian Tire veteran Mayne Plowman recalls thinking at the time.

They installed great long curving counters to serve the public. (In those days you didn't allow customers to wander the aisles by themselves.) But the place was so big it took salesmen ages to run around picking products off the shelves and to return to the front with them after they had taken an order. Muriel Billes, A.J.'s wife, had a solution: put the staff on roller skates. A.J. loved the idea. Soon salesmen were fairly flying about the place with all manner of piston rings, batteries and car accessories tucked under their arms or balanced precariously on their shoulders. Customers were delighted, not only with the

Service on a Roll

For many years, roller-skating clerks (*right and above*) were a popular feature of Canadian Tire's Yonge Street store. They provided speedy service within the large store along with a dash of entertainment. The clerks would write up an order at the front counter, and then race off to bring back the needed piston ring, battery or car accessory.

The earliest associate dealerships featured the Super-Lastic name rather than that of Canadian Tire, as views of the Weston, Ontario, store in 1939 (top right) and the London, Ontario, store in 1941 (far right) attest. Walker Anderson (shown bottom at left with A.J. Billes) opened the first Associate Dealership in Hamilton, Ontario, and was

soon followed by his enterprising sister-in-law, Agnes Anderson, whose Sudbury, Ontario, store is shown above. (Above right) the Chatham, Ontario, store in 1945.

faster service but also with the entertainment. Skate-propelled salesmen became expert at navigating the winding ramp that led to the service department or at scaling ladders to get at stock on the upper shelves.

The new store at 837 Yonge Street, for all its size and grandeur, was just a part of the Company's retailing empire. In 1934, J.W. had a brain wave: open other stores. Not branch stores, with managers who were employees, and would work only hard enough to get by. What he was looking for were associates — people who would have a personal stake in the business. With everything to gain — or lose — their level of energy and commitment should be limitless.

Walker Anderson was the first to buy in. In 1934 he opened the first Canadian Tire

Associate Store — a modest thirty by twenty-five foot outlet — on King Street in Hamilton, Ontario. He invested three thousand dollars in the business, most of which went toward stocking the shelves with the batteries, tires, tubes and bulk oil he bought from home office. The sign above the store read Super-Lastic Sales Corporation, not Canadian Tire, a way of giving prominence to the company tires.

There wasn't a contract between Canadian Tire and its Associate Dealers. A simple handshake sealed the deal. You agreed to buy only Canadian Tire products and to sell them at a prescribed price. For Walker and the great throng of dealers who quickly followed him, it was hard work. Among them was Walker's sister-in-law, Agnes Anderson, the company's first female Associate Dealer, who bought a dealership in Sudbury. They often worked alone

Word of Associate Dealerships quickly spread east to the Maritimes, where the Billes brothers' advertising had generated significant mail-order business. (Above left and right) The patriotic exterior and perfectly ordered interior of the Fredericton, New Brunswick, store in 1939.

Jack Canuck says—

CARS MUST LAST LONGER!

New car production has given way completely to the vastly more important job of building more and more war vehicles. You simply have to make your car last longer!

But . . . it isn't nearly as bad as it seems. Cars were built to last many tens of thousands of miles. It's our job to assist you in getting out of your car ALL the miles that were built into it.

"A STITCH IN TIME"

If you are one of those, who, in the past, neglected the proverbial "Stitch in time" —don't neglect those little things NOW. Today you can't banish the accumulation of neglect by "trading-it-in" on a new one.

Keeping cars on the road safely and economically has been our business for 28 years. Today we realise that we have a bigger job to do than ever before—and we'll do it if you'll give us the opportunity of being of service to you.

CANADIAN TIRE CORPORATION LIMITED 1943

TOWN

NAME THE COVER CONTEST (SEE INSIDE)

MAKE IT DO!

Replace ONLY where you cannot repair —buy only the most ESSENTIAL things—Make it do, wherever possible, for the duration.

A Stitch in Time!

"Spending a little to save a lot," however, is true war-time economy. The importance of keeping that ESSENTIAL vehicle of yours on the road, through prompt replacement of worn, dangerous parts, is recognized by both governments. High priorities to permit manufacture have been assigned to them. Such parts will be found listed throughout the pages that follow.

Not What it Used to Be!

Whether it be hardware, wearing apparel, auto supplies, furniture or almost any other commodity you name, it is NOT WHAT IT USED TO BE. This decline in quality is rarely the result of deliberate planning, but rather due to the necessity of substituting lesser materials for those considered critical. The depletion of skilled labour suffered by many plants, too, has contributed largely to this lessening of quality. So . . . if only due to the absence-of-quality and value-for-your-money angle, you should defer your buying until "after."

SHE AIN'T WHAT SHE USED TO BE

Surprise!

Yes, you will be surprised, pleased and amazed when the flood of new and improved products is released after the war's end. Mass war production methods will then be utilized to produce more and better materials at a much lower cost. Then you will be glad that you saved your money . . . that you, in the meantime, invested it in profitable War Bonds and War Savings Certificates . . . the safest and surest investment, available to every Canadian.

CANADIAN TIRE CORPORATION LIMITED SPRING & SUMMER 1942

MOTO-MASTER MUFFLER

NAME THE COVER CONTEST SEE PAGE 3

The spirit of the times is reflected in these wartime catalogues. Appeals to patriotism and self-sufficiency (above) exhort Canadians to "Make it Do." The covers (left) take a lighthearted look at life on the home front as two young men, one in army khaki and one in air force blue, poke fun at their dozing grandfather, who would soon evolve into Canadian Tire's advertising mascot.

to begin with, putting in one fourteen-hour day after another. Walker cooked his dinners on an oil heater in the garage. Mac McNish and Ed Leroy, co-owners of the first Ottawa store, slept under the counter for a time.

During World War II, conditions grew ever more difficult, regardless of whether Associates were firmly established or just setting up shop. Thousands of erstwhile drivers were enlisting in the armed forces. Gas, rubber and steel were rationed. Dealers had trouble stocking the shelves.

"Oh yes, we were affected," A.J. recalled. "More though in our inability to get merchandise than the difficulty in disposing of it."

Sandy MacDonald launched his North Bay, Ontario dealership in 1941 in a run-down wooden building at 239 Main Street East. "During that first winter, we changed our tires out on the streets, that's how much room there was.... I worked in that store from eight o'clock in the morning to eleven o'clock at night. My wife and I lived upstairs. There wasn't enough room to stand up, the ceiling was so low."

J.W.'s plan worked perfectly. From 1934 on, the expansion that followed was swift and sure. By 1945, just eleven years after Walker's store was opened, Canadian Tire boasted 110 stores. The retailer's successful mail-order business brought in many dealer inquiries. "We didn't go out to do it, to make Associates. The Associates came to us," A.J. recalled.

The Great Depression, followed by the war, didn't slow Canadian Tire down one bit. Indeed, during some of the very worst years of the Depression, business had increased — from $800,000 in 1933 to twice that in 1938. The company had everything going for it. The right products, the right prices, a wealth of price-conscious consumers, and a network of dealerships that didn't need a lot of careful care and feeding. As A.J. put it: "Give them the right products at the right price and success will follow." For all the successes of the period, however, even better times were on the way.

This now-famous photo shows a young boy bidding a last farewell to his papa, off to war from New Westminster, B.C., in 1940.

It Happened in the Thirties and Forties

W HEN THE HISTORY OF THE TWENTIETH century comes to be written, these two decades will surely rank as the most tumultuous. The Great Depression was a worldwide phenomenon, but many historians argue that few countries were harder hit than Canada. Everywhere the effects were similar: declining incomes and rising unemployment. Most countries tried to fight these by introducing tariffs to protect domestic industry, a strategy which prolonged and aggravated the world slump.

Economic hardship created political unrest, and Canada had its share of strikes and protests. Desperate for a way out, Canadians turned to new political parties that offered hope: in Alberta, they elected William Aberhart's Social Credit party; in Saskatchewan, Tommy Douglas and the CCF carried the day. In the United States, 1932 saw the election of Roosevelt with his promise of a New Deal. In Germany, Communists and National Socialists battled in the streets, and in 1933, Adolf Hitler was elected chancellor.

The "On to Ottawa" trek (above) began in British Columbia in 1935 as a protest against conditions in unemployment relief camps and the lack of a government-guaranteed minimum wage. The prairie drought (left) contributed to the hardships of the decade.

The growing importance of the car in Canadian life is clearly reflected in this 1940 catalogue cover (left). (Above) 1939 brought George VI and his consort, the present Queen Mother, to Canada in the first state visit to this country by a reigning monarch. (Below) "Black gold" was struck in the west, starting the oil boom which has continued to this day.

Hitler promised to make Germany great again, and proceeded to rearm. In September 1939, Germany invaded Poland. Once again, Canada was at war, although the Canadian declaration didn't come until September 10, 1939, a week later than Great Britain's, to show her independence.

During World War II, more than one million Canadians served in the Army, the Royal Canadian Navy or the Royal Canadian Air Force. The

Other significant events of the thirties and forties include:

• The Canadian Broadcasting Corporation was founded in 1936.

• Foster Hewitt broadcast his first game from Toronto's newly opened Maple Leaf Gardens in 1931.

• On May 24, 1934, Marie Dionne of Corbeil, Ontario, gave birth to Annette, Emilie, Yvonne, Cecile and Marie, soon to be world famous as the Dionne Quintuplets.

• Canadian troops landed in France as part of the disastrous Dieppe Raid in 1942. More than nine hundred were killed, and thirteen hundred taken prisoner. Canadian soldiers earned two Victoria Crosses.

• Gabrielle Roy published *Bonheur d'occasion* (*The Tin Flute*) in 1945. Ultimately translated into fifteen languages, it brought her instant literary fame.

Scenes from the thirties and forties: (top) a recruiting poster, (below) the Dionne quintuplets.

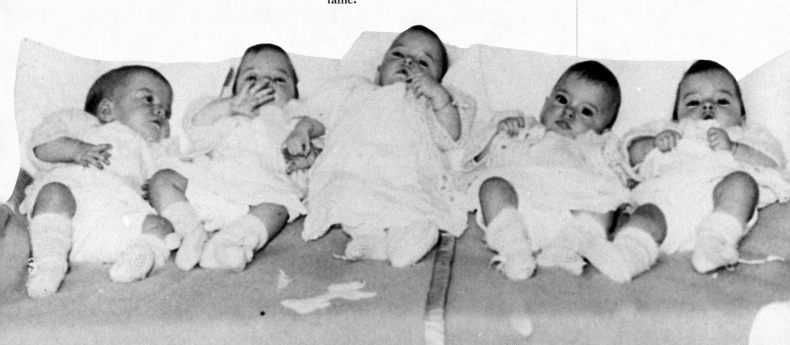

army fielded six divisions in Northern Europe, our navy was the third largest in the world by 1945, and the RCAF had forty-eight squadrons of bombers, fighters and transports fighting against Hitler. In all, 46,452 Canadians died in the fighting. In World War I, women had served in the forces and done traditional men's work in factories. But this time they were involved in far greater numbers both overseas and on the home front. Even children got in on the action, collecting scrap metal or searching the skies for elusive German or Japanese bombers. Canada also contributed technical expertise and uranium for the production of the atomic bomb.

(Above) A Montreal shopper studies rationing details. (Left) Canadians celebrate V-E Day. (Below) Joey Smallwood signs the agreement bringing Newfoundland into Confederation.

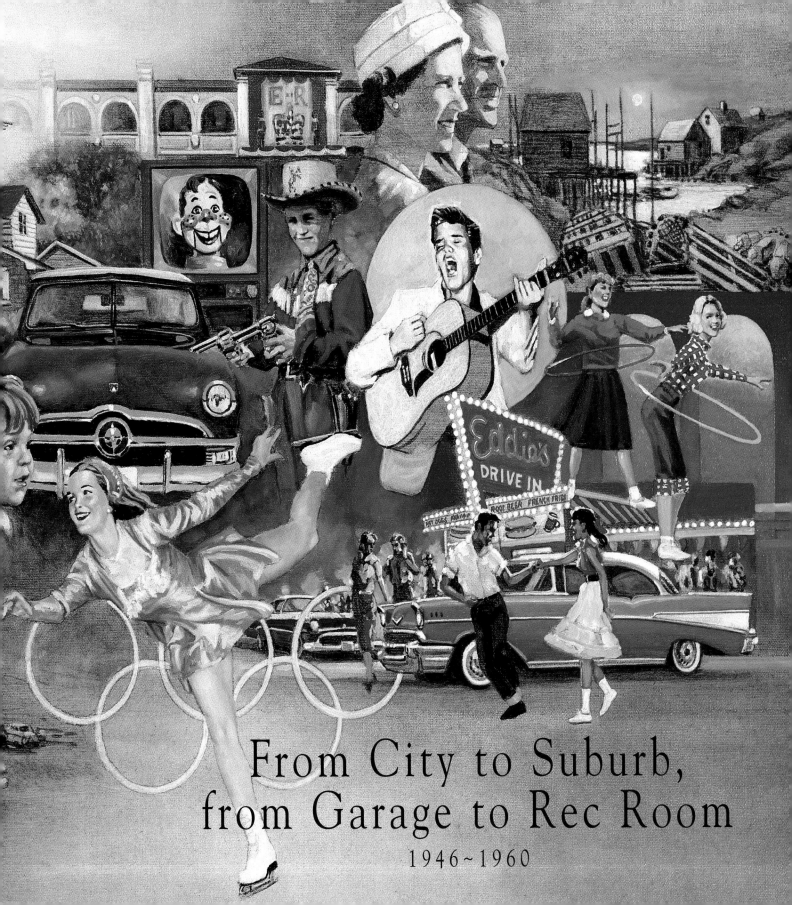

From City to Suburb,
from Garage to Rec Room

1946~1960

CHAPTER THREE

From City to Suburb, from Garage to Rec Room

1946~1960

I N 1945, CANADIANS HEAVED A COLLECTIVE SIGH OF relief as fifteen years of depression and war mercifully came to an end.

For a time, shortages of consumer goods persisted as the factories formerly pressed into wartime service returned to producing consumer goods. Until the late 1940s, in fact, Canadian Tire had trouble stocking its shelves. Tires, of all things, were among the products they were short of. If his tires were worn out, a driver could wait patiently for a new set or install re-liners — inserts that would buy you a few extra miles. But even these were hard to get. "I think we were probably taking all the manufacturer could make," A.J. recalled. "And every once in a while we'd advertise them and there'd be a block of people lined up waiting to get them."

With so little to sell, J.W. put the company's plans for expansion on hold through to the end of the 1940s. Still, the country's economic progress was steady and sure. As the 1940s gave way to what would later be called the Fabulous

(Below) Despite the postwar shortage of tires, Canadian ingenuity prevailed, as this tongue-in-cheek postcard implies. Once supplies became available, however, consumers rushed to Canadian Tire locations like the one in Sudbury, at right.

A Store Opening

The opening of a new store was big news in Bowmanville, Ontario (*bottom*), in 1959. Proprietor Stewart McTavish even issued invitations to the big event (*below*). On Friday evening the Bowmanville Legion Pipe Band led a group of majorettes (*top right*) and a parade of antique cars to the new store. After speeches by the mayor and Canadian Tire notables, the doors were thrown open. (*Right*) Customers streamed into the store while roses were distributed to the women and balloons handed out to the children.

ASSOCIATE STORE
160 CHURCH STREET,
BOWMANVILLE, ONT.

You are cordially invited to attend
Our Store Opening
Friday and Saturday, June 19th and 20th
Official ceremonies will take place
at 8:00 p.m. Friday evening.

C. Stewart McTavish,
PROPRIETOR.

...ian Statesman

...ounty's Great Family Journal

...ILLE, ONTARIO, THURSDAY, FEBRUARY 5th, 1959   10c Per Copy   NUM...

Canadian Tire Associate Stor...
Will Open in Simpkin Building...

Work Already Begun

Final approval was received on Tuesday for a Canadian Tire Associate Store to be constructed and operated in Bowman...

CANADIAN TIRE CORPⁿ

AUTOMNE-HIVER 1958-59

AUBAINES ALLÉCHANTES!

DO YOU SPEAK ENGLISH?
(SEE PAGE 4)

Canadian Tire in Quebec

Through the 1950s the network of Associate Dealers rapidly expanded through Ontario and eastward. After perusing a French language catalogue (*above and right*), Quebec shoppers could visit one of the sixteen Canadian Tire outlets in their province like the one in Hull (*top right*) or in Valleyfield (*centre right*).

Fifties, the country took off. Between 1945 and 1959, Canada's population increased by forty-three percent while disposable income jumped by a hundred and sixty-seven percent. Canadians of the 1950s were, indeed, among the wealthiest humans ever to have graced the planet. Canadian Tire, a company that prospered when times were tough, now fairly exploded with growth. Over the course of the 1950s, more than sixty new stores were added. The lion's share of them went to Ontario, but the ranks of the Maritime dealers swelled from ten to twenty-five, and a four-store toehold in Quebec grew to sixteen outlets, enough to justify publication of the company's first French-language catalogue in 1957. By 1959, Canadian Tire boasted one hundred and ninety retail outlets spread across Eastern Canada. Remarkably, all this expansion was done without borrowing a dime. Part of the money came from A.J. and J.W. themselves. Drawing modest wages (at least in comparison to today's captains of industry), they continually reinvested their profits in the business. Additional capital came from the stock market — from both J.W.'s own lucrative dealings in it during the war and from his decision to take Canadian Tire public in 1944, when a total of one hundred thousand common shares were issued, initially at a price of ten dollars each.

J.W. (top) and A.J. (above) Billes as they appeared in the 1950s. (Left) A.J. and his wife, Muriel, attend one of the many store openings that took place in this active decade.

Go East

Easteners, already in the habit of shopping at Canadian Tire by catalogue, were among the first to benefit from the

store's rapid eastward expansion in the 1950s. Associate Dealerships sprang up in Digby, Nova Scotia (top left), Sussex, New Brunswick (top right), St. John's, Newfoundland (left), and Yarmouth, Nova Scotia (above).

Ontario Stores

The growth that began in Ontario continued through the 1950s, with stores opening in Orangeville (top left), Paris (top right), Walkerton (middle right) and Forest (below). By this time Canadian Tire had become a family affair. Jack Spillette, shown bottom at right, became Newmarket's Associate Dealer in 1952, after the death of his father, dealer J.L. Spillette. Today Jack's son Peter carries on the tradition at his own dealership in Victoria, B.C.

(Above) *The company newsletter helped to foster a sense of community among the widely spread Associate Dealers.*
(Right) *The year 1954 saw Canadian Tire's first "pin-party" to honour those with 25 years of service. A.J. and J.W. both received pins, as did longtime employee Norm Jones, seen here.*
(Below) *The proud crew at the Niagara Falls, Ontario, store.*

Apparently investors liked the stock. By 1952 shares were going for thirty dollars.

The employees were a source of money, too. In 1946, A.J. and J.W. had replaced the old informal bonus system — a little here, a little there — with a scheme that saw ten percent of a worker's wages withheld, invested in the company and paid back ten years later, with interest. (In 1956, employees were given the option of buying shares in Canadian Tire. And thanks to the skyrocketing value of Canadian Tire stock — a share initially worth $8.50 ballooned to $4,900.00 by 1987 — many became rich. Jimmy Douglas, a floor sweeper, received several hundred thousand dollars the day he hung up his broom.)

Every issue of the company newsletter seemed to have news of a store opening or expanding. In the many small communities Canadian Tire was now serving, these openings were often the biggest show in town. In the October 1953 edition of the *Mouthpiece*, the company newsletter, North Bay dealer Sandy MacDonald recounted his visit to the grand opening of Vic Muncaster's "big new store" in Sault Ste. Marie.

Taking to the Ice

Inspired by the 1948 Olympic victory of Canadian skating sensation Barbara Ann Scott, thousands of young girls (*top and above*) laced up and took to the ice. Billing ice sports as "a ton 'o fun for everyone," Canadian Tire offered everything for skaters and hockey players, young and old (*right*). The store also offered skate sharpening services (*below*).

Skating... a ton o' fun for everyone!

11.95 Pair
6.98
14.95
24.50
19.95
13.95
4.99 Pair

1 **Feature Value** — The Mastercraft "Extra Special". A quality outfit made by Daoust-Lalonde. Built-in tendon guards, armored toe caps, leather interling and padded tongue. Fine, full-grain-leather uppers. Riveted to speedy "St. Lawrence" tube skates. Sizes 5 to 12.
No. S 2193X—State size. Worth 15.00 .... **11.95**

2 **Low-Priced Pleasure or Hockey Outfits**—Sturdy black pebble-grain leather uppers, waterproof rubber soles and excellent quality tube skates. Tendon guards, sewn-in web reinforcement for firm ankle support. Felt padded tongue. State size.
No. S 1111X—Boys' sizes 11-2. Pair **6.98**
No. S 1173X—Men's sizes 3-12. Pair **7.98**

Mastercraft "Semi-Pro" Hockey Outfit—(Not shown). Fine top-grain leather uppers in black, with handsome tan-colored toe caps and trim. Cross-stitched full leather lining, felt-padded tongues, waterproof soles and built-in tendon guards. High grade, satin-finish tube skates with specially hardened blades. Men's sizes 3-12.
No. S 1174X—State size. Worth 16.50 .... **9.75**

3 **Men's "Daoust Lalonde" Special Hockey Outfit**. Has all the fine features of outfits costing much more. Black, top-quality grain-leather uppers with cross-stitched leather lining. Built-in tendon guards, padded tongue. Leather soles. Contrasting Red leather trim. Riveted to excellent quality tube skates with specially hardened blades. Worth 18.00!
No. S 894X—Men's sizes 5 to 13. Pair **14.95**

4 **"Samson" De Luxe Outfit** — Professional-built with flexible, leather-covered steel tendon guards. Arch-support insole, steel shank, spring heel. Beautiful, smooth grain-leather uppers, cross-stitched leather lining. Box toes, cut-off professional-type soles. Firmly riveted to de luxe tube skates.
No. S 1176X—Sizes 5 to 12. Pair **19.95**

5 **"Samson" Super Hockey Outfit** — Our best quality. With features of outfits selling for up to 57.00! Double-helmet toes, Celastic counter, comfortable sponge interlining, plus English kip-leather lining. "Ace-Pro" tube skates with hardened steel blades.
No. S 880X—Sizes 6 to 12. Pair **24.50**

6 **Men's "Professional-Type" Hockey Outfit** — Black grain-leather uppers with tan leather-trim, leather soles. Heavily-padded tongue, double-reinforced eyelets, cross-stitched leather lining; fracture-proof, built-in tendon guards; top quality tube skates.
No. S 911X—Sizes 5 to 12. Pair **13.95**

7 **Beginners' Tube-Skate Outfit** — For 3 to 7 years. Strong, hockey-style leather boots with built-in ankle support, outside strap and buckle. "Easy-to-stand-on" semi-tube skates. Sizes 7 to 11. State size.
No. S 1195X—Girls' white boots;
No. S 1196X—Boys' black boots **4.99**
SPECIAL "Dunne" Adjustable Bob Skates.
No. S 996—For the "small-fry". Pair .... **.98**

ALL-WHITE . . . 1st CHOICE FOR THE LADIES

11.98 Pair
6.98 Pair
7.98 Pair

8 **"All-White" Skating Outfit**—Sparkling white "elk" fine grain leather with ankle supports; weatherproof white rubber sole. Smartly shaped, comfortable tops. Fitted with handsome tube skates.
No. S 1053X—Misses' sizes 11 to 2. Pair **6.98**
No. S 1054X—Women's sizes 3 to 9. Pair **7.98**

9 **"All-White" Pleasure Skating Outfit with "Figure Skates"**— Moderately priced for those who want figure skates for ordinary rink skating. High white boot with shaped top. Welt leather sole. Fitted with chrome-plated figure skates. (No half-sizes.)
No. S 1078X— ... sizes 11 to 2. Pair **7.98**
No. ... 's sizes 3 to 9. Pair **8.98**

... ra-Special" — All-white figure or pleasure ... gain price for a really high quality product— ... Full grain-leather uppers, soft kip-leather lining. ... ng counter. Contrasting black soles and heels. ... me-plated figure skates of professional design. ... to 9. State size on order.
... 0. Only, per pair. **11.98**

... Skating Outfit — "Instructor approved". ... glish figure skates. This outfit will ideally ... gure skating lessons. Solid leather heels. ... padded ankle and tongue. Lined with ... ly-shaped combination narrow-heel last. ... o to 9½ (including half-sizes) **16.95**

Crowds thronged the store, he reported, perhaps drawn by door prizes that included "a shotgun, sun visor, electric kettle, polishing kit, auto robe, seat covers, tire or battery, combination spotlamp, two gallons of paint and a tricycle." A total of 2,500 hats and 3,600 balloons were given out at the three-day event, not to mention a free rose to the first seventy-five "ladies in the store," one of whom included Vic's brother Laird, clad in women's clothing, ostensibly to get a rose for his wife. "Laird got his rose even if his cheeks got a little pink in doing it," the *Mouthpiece* reported.

For Canadian Tire's oldest dealers, those who had cut their teeth during the difficult years of the 1930s and early 1940s, the 1950s were magical. "A lot of water has gone under the bridge since 1942," Sandy MacDonald wrote in 1952. "From our $2,800 stock (of merchandise) that started us in business, we now have approximately $50,000. We don't live over the store anymore, we own a house. We have a car and a half-ton truck. All through our association with C.T.C."

Success created its own problems. Throughout the early fifties, Canadian Tire was plagued by a shortage of storage space, a problem relieved only temporarily over the years by constructing a five-storey warehouse behind the main store. Later the company purchased a building at 940 Yonge Street and, after that, the 86,000-square-foot Canada Bread factory nearby. But a chain with more than 150 stores needed a proper warehouse. On November 13, 1956, J.W.'s wife Gladys drove a gold-plated spade into the frozen ground of a forty-one-acre parcel of land in north Toronto. It marked the start of construction on the Sheppard Avenue Warehouse, a sprawling 225,000-square-foot facility that opened the following year.

J.W. himself couldn't attend the ground-breaking. He'd entered the hospital the day before with breathing problems and welts up and down his arms. He died three days later as a result of complications from pernicious anemia, caused, his doctors believed, by the drugs he'd taken sometime before for pneumonia. Just a month and a half shy of sixty, he left an estate worth a little over six million dollars. "He worked too hard and played too hard," his brother said.

Growth of the Canadian Tire network quickly outpaced available storage space, and by the mid-fifties it was clear that expanded facilities were needed. The ground-breaking ceremony for the new North Toronto warehouse was eagerly awaited (above). A.J. Billes and J.W.'s wife, Gladys, did the honours (below). Sadly, J.W. was too ill to attend and did not live to see the opening of the new facility in 1957 (right).

A Home for Every Family

As Canadians moved from city centres to the suburbs that were rapidly springing up all over the country (*above*), their thoughts turned to enhancing their new homes, inside and out. From paintbrushes to workbenches, Canadian Tire provided everything the do-it-yourselfer (*top right*) could need. A page from the 1960 Spring/Summer catalogue (*right*) offered gardening tools for the whole family.

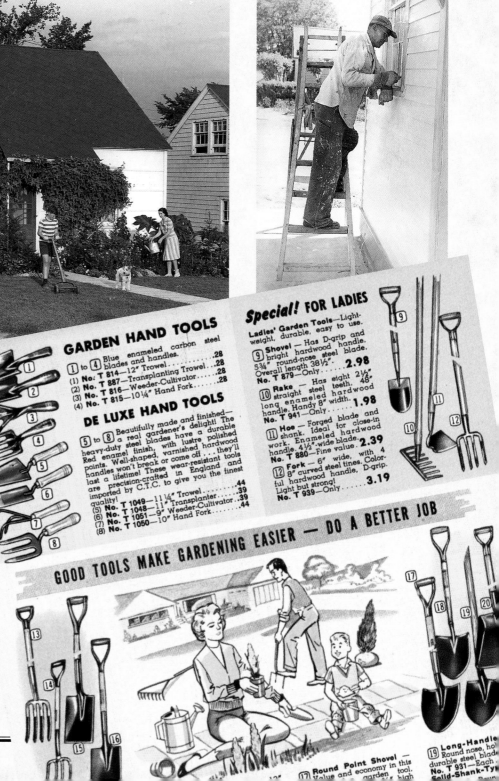

GARDEN HAND TOOLS

① to ④ Blue enameled carbon steel blades and handles............28
(1) No. T 814—12" Trowel...........28
(2) No. T 887—Transplanting Trowel...28
(3) No. T 816—Weeder-Cultivator....28
(4) No. T 815—10¼" Hand Fork.......28

DE LUXE HAND TOOLS

⑤ to ⑧ Beautifully made and finished! The real gardener's delight! The heavy-duty steel blades have a durable Red enamel finish, with lustre polished points. Well-shaped, varnished hardwood handles won't break or come off ... they'll last a lifetime! These wear-resistant tools are precision-crafted in England and imported by C.T.C. to give you the finest quality!
(5) No. T 1049—11¼" Trowel.........44
(6) No. T 1048—11" Transplanter.....39
(7) No. T 1051—9" Weeder-Cultivator..44
(8) No. T 1050—10" Hand Fork.......44

Special! FOR LADIES

Ladies' Garden Tools—Light-weight, durable, easy to use.
⑨ Shovel — Has D-grip and bright hardwood handle. 5¾" round-nose steel blade. Overall length 38½". No. T 879—Only.......**2.98**
⑩ Rake — Has eight 2½" straight steel teeth, 48" long enameled hardwood handle. Handy 8" width. No. T 941—Only.......**1.98**
⑪ Hoe — Forged blade and shank. Ideal for close-in work. Enameled hardwood handle. 4½"-wide blade. No. T 880—Fine value..**2.39**
⑫ Fork — 6" wide, with 4 8" curved steel tines. Colorful hardwood handle, D-grip. Light but strong! No. T 939—Only.......**3.19**

GOOD TOOLS MAKE GARDENING EASIER — DO A BETTER JOB

⑰ **Round Point Shovel** — Value and economy in this garden tool. High

⑲ **Long-Handle** Round nose, ho durable steel blade No. T 931—Each Solid-Shank-Ty

J.W. ran his company as a chess player might have — he was detached and withdrawn, but he had a passion for strategy and the details. For all his success, he used to come to Mayne Plowman's office on occasion and say, "I'd just love it if we still had a little store on Yonge Street."

A.J. took over as president at once. Following a simple management philosophy, "It's a matter of the plain old saying, do unto others as you would have others do unto you, and you can't go very far wrong," his style was distinctly different from that of his brother. He was less cautious, a risk-taker, and he wasted no time in launching initiatives J.W. would almost certainly have opposed. To begin with, Canadian Tire re-entered the retail gas business after an absence of thirty years by opening a gas bar outside the store at 837 Yonge St.

Selling gas in Toronto in the late 1950s looked to be a pretty lucrative business, or so A.J. thought at the time. It only made sense that Canada's largest automotive parts retailer should get in on the action. For a time, Canadian Tire gas was the best deal in the city. But the big oil companies hadn't left much room for independent gas retailers in Canada and they weren't about to leave any more. A.J. had to figure out how to attract customers without getting into a price war with the oil companies, a battle that even prosperous Canadian Tire couldn't win.

"The oil companies sold gas at a fantastic margin of profit," A.J later recalled. "I couldn't resist it, but I didn't dare cut prices." Instead, A.J. decided that if you paid cash for gas, you'd get five percent back in the form of Canadian Tire 'Money.' "I realized the only way you could compete was through cross-merchandising. But no one had ever done that." The 'Money' was a hit. One of the greatest innovations in the history of Canadian retailing was born.

The idea actually came from A.J.'s wife Muriel, the same woman who thought Moto-Master would make a great brand name for Canadian Tire automotive parts. She had also suggested two decades before that salesmen at the main store could serve customers far faster by wearing roller skates.

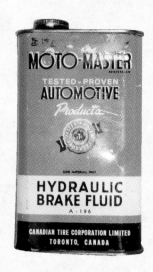

The continuing success of house-brand products encouraged the Billes brothers to expand the Moto-Master line. By the end of the 1950s, Moto-Master could supply a complete array of car-care products.

The first coupon series featured a piece of artwork that, even at that time, was a Canadian Tire classic — a happy tire and a dollar running along hand in hand above the slogan "We Make Your Dollars Go Farther." On the back was, improbably, a combined rural-industrial scene with a Canadian Tire store seeming to hold in its orbit a train, ship, airplane and cars — a visual metaphor for the Canadian economy with a bustling Canadian Tire store at its physical and spiritual centre.

The paper quality was poor at first. Once folded, the bills tended to fall apart. But fragility begets rarity and value, and among avid collectors of Canadian Tire 'Money' today, the fifty-cent coupon from these first so-called "Rural Scene" notes is the ultimate possession. "In brand-new condition," says Roger Fox, who today leads the 235 members of the Canadian Tire Coupon Collectors Club, "one traded a year ago for five hundred dollars."

In 1961, the next generation of 'Money' was issued in the store and redeemable with either cash purchases of gas or store goods. It was printed on genuine bank-note paper by the British American Bank Group, no less, printers of Canadian currency. This was A.J.'s master stroke, a touch of tactile wizardry. Because the coupons felt like real money, they were psychologically just about impossible to throw away — and just about as durable a piece of advertising as any company could hope for.

The store 'Money' featured the immortal Sandy McTire, as drawn by Canadian Tire artist Bernie Freedman. With his ruddy complexion, thick upturned moustache and jaunty tam-'o-shanter, Sandy was the very picture of robust good cheer. With a few strokes of the pen, Freedman created an archetype of a genial bargain hunter and a potent symbol for the retailer's central message: discerning buyers, Scotsmen or not, know Canadian Tire's the place to shop.

But Canadian Tire promotions in the 1950s weren't confined to the 'Money' alone. The retailer was famous for its larger-than-life storefront displays at Yonge and Davenport.

In the late 1950s, Canadian Tire developed one of its greatest promotional ideas, one that continues to work to this day: Canadian Tire 'Money.' The "rural scene" note (middle and bottom) was the first design of the 'Money' ever issued.

To commemorate Queen Elizabeth's coronation on June 2, 1953, a crown, eight feet high and twenty-five feet in circumference, was constructed of wood and papier-mâché and placed above the main entrance. A total of 316 lights were laid on top to give a jewel-encrusted effect. Meanwhile, two life-size Grenadier Guard statues stood protectively on either side of the crown. For Christmas 1956, a colossal Santa was erected. Seventy-two feet high, with a thirty-foot waistline, he took a size eighty-four boot.

In the booming fifties, Canadian Tire became one of the largest retailers in the country. The company had lost its cofounder, but under A.J. Billes's energetic stewardship, Canadian Tire was on the verge of greatness. All that was needed was a push westward, beyond the Ontario border, and input — modern business techniques, systems and methods — from the sharp young minds being produced by the management schools springing up all over the continent.

1953: Coronation Fever

In 1953 Canadians greeted the crowning of Elizabeth II (*right*) with widespread enthusiasm. For the first time, millions were able to view the ceremony on television. Within hours of the coronation it was broadcast nationwide on the CBC, thanks to the cooperation of the air force, which rushed film shot at Westminster Abbey to Canada by fighter jet. Like everyone else, Canadian Tire was swept up in coronation excitement. The flagship Yonge Street store (*above*) was decked out especially for the event with the new sovereign's monogram and an excellent reproduction of the coronation crown, flanked by two red-coated guardsmen.

Owning a Car in the Fifties

The economic boom of the fifties and sixties brought many Canadians the kind of prosperity they had only dreamed about before the war. Their material success was expressed through their vehicles, and an unprecedented number were taking to the road, as the view above of a 1956 traffic jam demonstrates.

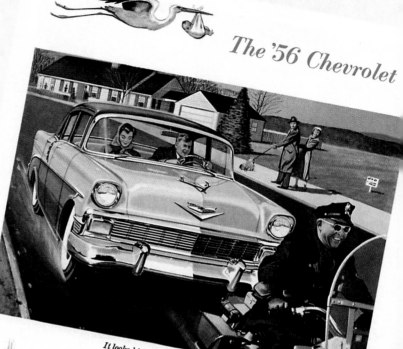

The '56 Chevrolet

It looks high priced—but it's the new Chevrolet "Two-Ten" 4-Door Sedan

...r sooner and safer arriva...

...t's so nimble and quick on the road ...

...f course, you don't have to have an urgent ...rand and a motorcycle escort to make use of ...hevrolet's quick and nimble ways. Wherever ...you go, the going's sweeter and safer in a Chevy.

...Power's part of the reason. Chevrolet's horse-...power ranges up to 205. And these numbers add ...p to *action*—second-saving acceleration for ...fer passing ... rapid-fire reflexes that help ...u avoid trouble before it happens!

...ots of cars are high powered today, but ...ence is in the way Chevrolet *handles* ...l. It's rock-steady on the road ... ...rves like part of the pavement. ...ity—and it helps make Chevrolet ... great road cars!

...e, soon. Your Chevrolet dealer ... arrange it. . . . Chevrolet ...l Motors, Detroit 2, Mich.

THE HOT ONE'S EVEN ...

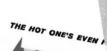

Traffic-... it's a beaut... to han...

Exciting N...

① **"Lo-Boy"** Palm Grip Hugs the steering wheel a... steering control. Lustrous plastic combination.
No. A 1599—Neatly styled...

② **"Stylized"** Wheel Spi... to fit your hand. Beauti... plastic knob with contrastin... Bright chrome base.
No. A 1074—Real value...

③ **"Artists' Models"** W... —Eye-captivating "Pi... gorgeously presented und... lens. Take your pick of b... or redheads—in tantalizi... Rich Tenite knob with ... chrome base.
No. A 1949—Each......

Super-DeLuxe "Kodac... Girls—Actual color pho... models—completely cap...
No. A 2006—Each......

AUTO...

Speed and safety were the primary selling features of the enormous 1956 Chevrolet (above). (Left) This illustration from another period advertisement makes a shiny new car seem like one of the family.

DO IT YOURSELF!

FREE KNOW HOW

Car enthusiasts in the fifties took great pride in customizing and repairing their own vehicles (above). Even the wheel spinners in the 1954 catalogue (below) promised excitement.

Winter in Canada sometimes seems to last forever, defying even a snowplough's best efforts (above). For particularly frosty mornings, Canadian Tire offered engine heaters to get you started and tire chains to help "stop that skid" (top and bottom right).

STOP THAT SKID

Save Safely on SUPER QUALITY

TIRE CHAINS

For all CARS and TRUCKS

HEEL SPINNERS

④ **"Full-Chrome" Wheel Spinner**— Base and body are fully triple-plated in mirror-bright chrome; translucent plastic top glows with gem-like beauty.
No. A 1962—Each........................ **1.10**

⑤ **Hand Carved Matched "Rose" Spinner and Gear Shift Knob**— Beautifully life-like! Sculptured in high-relief to provide a genuine 3rd-dimension. Exquisitely hand colored by skilled artists. Shimmering Lucite; chrome base.
No. A 2224—Complete set........ **1.95**

"Rose" Spinner only—
No. A 2121—Each.................... **1.19**

⑥ **"Out-O-Way" Spinner**—This precision safe driving instrument features a comfortable plastic knob and streamlined sparkling chrome base. At slight pressure on convenient button the knob springs out of driving position—Clicks back instantly when wanted.
No. A 1950—Each.................... **2.15**

GEARSHIFT CONTROL KNOBS

⑦ **Gearshift Knob**— For conventional control. Rich Tenite, pear shaped. (Less bushing).
No. A 1075...... **.27**

Moulded rubber—
No. A 1616...... **.14**

⑧ **Steering Column Shift Lever Knob** —Replace present knob on 1939-53 cars with colorful marbelized plastic. (Give make of car, etc. (Less bushing).
No. A 1078...... **.29**

No. A 1413—Fits Chevrolet, 1940-48; (no bushing needed)........ **.34**

⑨ **Bushings**—To adapt gearshift knobs. Give complete car information.
No. A 1080—Rubber bushing........ **.06**
No. A 1081 X—Brass bushing........ **.12**

CKS and HANDLES — TRUNK HINGES

andles to replace original equipment. lars, also exact location of handle you ⑮ **Glove Compartment Locks**—Give full vehicle particulars and quote Cat. No. A 46X.

Chevrolet and most Pontiac, Buick and Oldsmobile 1940-54 .... **1.75**
1936-39........................ **2.10** Chrysler, Plymouth, Dodge and DeSoto—1941-54 .... **1.39**

Chrysler, Plymouth, Dodge and DeSoto—1936-39. original equipment. Complete

Pillar Locks—Replacing original equipment. Complete car data and Cat. No. A 46X. **2.39**

The growth of suburbia through the fifties and sixties (below) meant that both Mom and Dad needed their own cars to get around. Canadian Tire was quick to acknowledge this trend by providing "Everything for the two-car family," in this catalogue from the early sixties (right). (Above) A service bay in Hull, Quebec.

CANADIAN TIRE CORP'N
FALL AND WINTER 1962-63

EVERYTHING FOR
The **TWO-CAR** FAMILY

CANADIAN TIRE CORP'N

PARLEZ-VOUS FRANÇAIS?
(VOIR PAGE 6)

The family car brought with it infinite possibilities for motoring holidays. (Above) Tourists are greeted at Keltic Lodge, Nova Scotia. (Below) A growing number of auto holiday-makers meant a surge in the number of highway motels.

It Happened in the Forties and Fifties

For most Canadians, the fifteen years after the end of the Second World War were a time when life was better than anyone could ever remember. New subdivisions snaked out from the old cities, fast covering farmland in Don Mills, Burnaby and

Other notable events of the immediate postwar years:

• Between 1946 and 1960, nearly one and a half million people entered Canada. Many were part of the great army of refugees created by war and the spread of Communism; others, part of the ebullient wave of Italians, Greeks and other Europeans headed for Canada's major cities.

• In sports, Barbara Ann Scott won a gold medal in figure skating at the 1948 St. Moritz Winter Games. A plucky sixteen-year-old, Marilyn Bell, became the first person ever to swim across Lake Ontario in September 1954. The Montreal Canadiens won the Stanley Cup six times, 1952-53, 1954-55, 1955-56, 1957-58, 1958-1959 and 1959-60. And in 1958, George Chuvalo, arguably the greatest Canadian boxer ever, won the Canadian heavyweight crown for the first time.

(Bottom) A Hungarian family dines at a refugee reception center in 1956. Newsmakers of the forties and fifties included: Marilyn Bell (left); Mackenzie King (below); the cast of Country Hoedown *(opposite left), starring a youthful Tommy Hunter, seen at center with guitar; and Paul Anka (opposite right).*

Montreal's West Island. In this new Canada, the car was king. Once, owning a car had been only a dream, but now many people felt they needed two: one, so Dad could drive to work, and another so Mom could take the children to school, hockey or ballet, stopping off on the way at one of the new shopping malls that were springing up everywhere.

In 1948, Canada's longest-serving prime minister, Mackenzie King, resigned in favour of the avuncular Louis St. Laurent. Out of office, King, often dismissed during his life as a colourless figure, could dedicate more time to his other great interest: communing with the spirit of his dead mother, the ghost of his beloved dog Rex and other assorted departed friends. In 1957, the Liberal government fell to John Diefenbaker, a fiery Prairie populist Conservative. In the subsequent election in 1958 Diefenbaker won with what was at the time the largest landslide ever — not just in Canadian history, but in any democracy on Earth.

• Rock'n'roll was born, and rapidly spread worldwide. The foremost Canadian practitioner of the new form was Ottawa's Paul Anka, who recorded such hits as "Diana," "Lonely Boy," and "You Are my Destiny."

• Television came to Canada. A Montreal CBC station was the first to broadcast commercially, on Sept. 6, 1952. The Toronto station followed two days later. Popular programs from the early years included *Hockey Night in Canada*, *Juliette* (which followed the hockey game), and *The Plouffes*, which had the distinction of going out twice each week, in French on Radio-Canada on Wednesday, then on CBC in English on Friday.

1867 | 1967

FLOWER POWER

Years
of Change

1961~1980

CHAPTER FOUR

Years of Change

1961~1980

ALTHOUGH COLD WAR TENSIONS DOMINATED THE international scene, in retrospect, the early 1960s seem like years of relative tranquillity and contentment in Canada.

But Canadian Tire was waging a small war of its own —

a price war. The large oil companies had not taken kindly to the prospect of Canadian Tire gas bars springing up in almost every town and city in central Canada. So the gloves came off and price-cutting began in earnest.

Facing some stiff opposition, A.J. Billes produced a

special "gas war" coupon, redeemable only when prices rose above forty-nine cents a gallon. The front showed a mountainous Herculean figure preparing to smash with ball and chain the humble Canadian Tire gas bar that lay at his feet. On the back, A.J. issued a call to arms: "With your help, together we will defy the giants and win the gas war. Standing alone, pitted against giants, C.T.C. hasn't a chance, but — shoulder to shoulder with you, the customer — we will win this war. Our mutual cause is morally and economically right."

The war escalated. In June 1960, the oil companies stopped supplying gas to the retailer. A.J. responded by buying sixty million gallons of gas from the Soviet Union — "cold war gas" it was called — while pressing forward relentlessly with plans to build gas bars throughout the chain. The war cost a fortune (at its height, one Canadian Tire gas bar was losing $25,000 a week), but a year later, there were 31 gas bars either built or in the works. When the guns fell silent and the smoke cleared, Canadian Tire was still in the retail gas business. Today, there are 194 gas bars across Canada.

The Quebec City gas bar and store (left) are shown decked out for Canada's Centennial. The "gas war" coupon (above) dates from the early 1960s, when major oil companies battled Canadian Tire for customers by cutting prices. Consumers were encouraged to think of themselves as an army of Davids helping Canadian Tire fight against the Goliath-like oil companies.

One of Canadian Tire's proudest moments: A.J. Billes is presented with the Order of Canada (below). This honour (right) was bestowed in recognition of his innovative work in profit sharing. He felt that Canadian Tire's employees should be rewarded for the part they played in the company's success.

Victory in the gas wars was one of A.J.'s greatest achievements. By squaring off with the oil companies, he had secured a position in a market that he had known very little about at first and had helped take Canadian Tire to ninety-seven million dollars in sales by the mid-sixties. Earlier he had been clever enough to see that the promotional value of Canadian Tire 'Money' far outweighed its considerable cost, and his convictions were strong enough to take a wild idea and see it through to implementation.

Then, in 1965, A.J.'s doctor told him he was developing stress-related diabetes. Carrying on as president could cost him his health, perhaps even his life, so he decided to step down. Although he gave up the reins to the company in 1966, A.J. went to work almost every day for the rest of his life. For a time he ran the tire department, his favourite part of the business. And from his seat on the Board of Directors, which he held until 1988, he promoted profit sharing tirelessly. Largely because of his pioneering work in this field, A.J. received the Order of Canada in 1976.

In appointing a successor, A.J. didn't have to look far to find a thirty-two-year-old wunderkind by the name of Joseph Dean Muncaster. Dean was no stranger to retailing or to Canadian Tire, since his father Walter was one of the finest of the first-generation dealers. One of seven brothers raised on a farm in Northern Ontario, Walter Muncaster left school after grade eight. In 1939, he got a job managing Agnes Anderson's Canadian Tire store in Sudbury. Six years later, he bought the

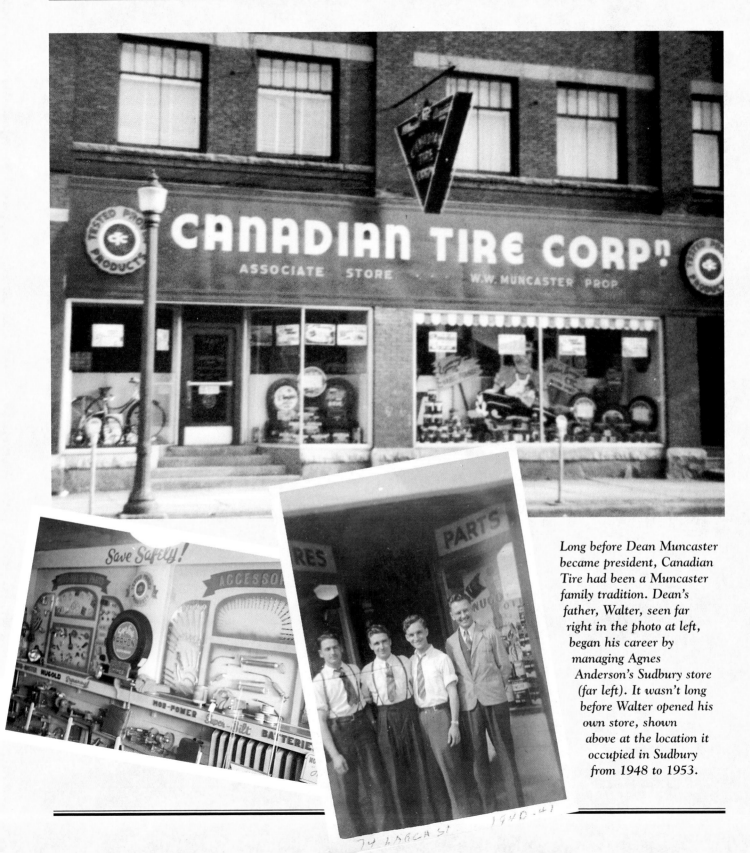

Long before Dean Muncaster became president, Canadian Tire had been a Muncaster family tradition. Dean's father, Walter, seen far right in the photo at left, began his career by managing Agnes Anderson's Sudbury store (far left). It wasn't long before Walter opened his own store, shown above at the location it occupied in Sudbury from 1948 to 1953.

The explosion of affluence in the 1960s made fully equipped wilderness adventures available — and desirable — to nearly everyone. The interior of the 1968 catalogue (*below*) displayed a dazzling array of portable shelters, while the cover (*right*) featured a sleek, modern home-away-from-home, complete with every convenience. Compare this idyllic view with the more rustic fishing trip promised by the 1941 catalogue cover on page 37.

CANADIAN TIRE

PRINTEMPS-ÉTÉ 1968

Pièces et accessoires d'automobile, quincaillerie, articles de sport, etc.

Voir pages 194-195 pour des remorques de "Knight"

TENTES *Mastercraft*

129.95

89.95

49.98

① **Petite te**...
gris perle...
démonte très...
76-5002—Fc...

② **Tente**...
à tête d'...
Avec mât e...
76-5004—...

③ **Tent**...
En ti...
et jaune...
à moustiqua...
Environ 7 x 7...
Mât central réglable,...
dispens... beaucoup d'om...
76-5023—Avec mâts, piquets et hau...

④ **Tente touriste à armature extérieu**...
plaire. L'armature extérieure réglable, en de...
dégage l'intérieur et élimine les mâts et piquets, s...
l'auvent. La tente s'attache à l'armature et un double to...
couleur se fixe dessus. Grand auvent festonné, pleine largeur.
Porte hollandaise à seuil à glissière et rabat extérieur à cordons. 2 poches; tapis de sol cousu. Tissu imputrescible au fini à sec Durafin.
76-5049—9 x 9 x 7 pi. 3 peuvent y coucher........... **64.50**

Tente touriste normale—Même genre que ci-dessus mais sans armature extérieure. Beaucoup d'espace au sol et en hauteur. Une tente vraiment économique.
76-5026—9 x 9 x 6½ pi. Avec mâts, piquets, etc...... **35.95**

Tente touriste de luxe—Tous les avantages de tentes coûtant bien plus cher. Élégante; murs en épais coutil hydrofuge; épais tapis de sol cousu; toit très épais en toile. Une splendide tente, facile à monter et à prix-réclame.
76-5037—9 x 9 x 7½ pi. Avec mâts, piquets acier... **44.95**

⑤ **Familiale Campani IV**—4 adultes y couchent à l'aise. Grande porte avant à glissière; épais sol caoutchouté Molino, cousu. Grande fenêtre arrière à moustiquaire nylon et rabat extérieur à cordons. Fait 8 x 7 x 6 pi.
76-5038—Avec mâts, piquets et haubans............ **59.95**

⑥ **Tente normale à hauts murs**—6 personnes y couchent à l'aise. 2 fenêtres à moustiquaire de chaque côté. Porte hollandaise déportée; auvent pleine largeur; 4 poches intérieures. Toit en toile de 11 oz. et murs en coutil de 9½ oz. après traitement; épais sol cousu. 10 x 12 x 7½ pi.
76-5055—Avec mâts, piquets, haubans et auvent.... **89.95**

⑩ **Tente famili**...
face de 9 x 18' con...
pièces séparées. 7 personnes p...
séjour de 9 x 12. Fenêtres plein...
hollandaise à moustiquaire vinyle-nylo...
rabats à cordons de tous côtés; 4 poches; é...
Abri-salle à manger de 6 x 9' à moustiquaires vinyle...
Portes à glissière pleine longueur entre les 2 pièces.
Toit en épaisse toile de 15 oz. après traitement. Murs en cou... serré de 11 oz. après traitement. Avec mâts réglables, pique... en acier et instructions de montage.
76-5059—Fait 9 x 18 x 7½ pi. de haut............ **139.9**

⑪ **Tentes à pans de style européen** pour ceux qui veule... une tente **moderne, différente** et très supérieure. No... avons une grandeur et un style à la portée de tous. **Rense... gnez-vous auprès de votre marchand Canadian Tire**.

⑫ **Toit ou coupe-vent de camping**—Peut servir de tent... d'abri pour manger ou à bagages. Livré avec 6 mâts, piquets, 6 haubans et des tendeurs. 12 x 10 pi.
76-5219—Coutil havane de 11 oz. Seulement........ **25.9**

Des mâts en acier, sacs à mâts, sacs à piquets et piquet... se trouvent chez votre marchand Canadian Tire.

The transition from city life to wilderness adventure was a snap when you hauled your tent behind you and could set up anywhere. Or you could set up right in your own backyard (opposite right). Cottage life in decades past (left and right). Today the Kenora, Ontario, store (above) is completely accessible to water traffic.

Dressed like a stewardess, that symbol of 1960s female freedom and sophistication, Miss Mor Power gave Canadian Tire gas and automotive products an attractive, modern face.

dealership with seven thousand dollars he scraped together and another six thousand lent to him by J.W. Billes. Over the next few years, Walter became the model for every other Canadian Tire dealer to follow. In 1956, his store became the first to reach one million dollars a year in sales, and a short time later, the first to tear down the front counter and let customers walk among the merchandise. He was also one of the founders of the Canadian Tire Dealers Association.

Almost from the moment he bought the store, Walter's family was helping him to run it. On Saturdays and after school, Dean was at his father's side, stocking shelves, helping customers and assisting in the service department. "My father and I were very close. He was a mentor to me," Dean recalls.

Thus grounded in retailing's fundamentals, Dean went on to earn, not one, but two business degrees: the first, an undergraduate degree in business from the University of Western Ontario in London, Ontario; the second, a Masters in Business Administration from prestigious Northwestern University in the United States.

In the 1950s, business schools were still a new idea. The days when clerks, floor sweepers, miners and brakemen could start at the bottom and rise to the top were swiftly coming to an end. The white-collar work force was being invaded by smart, young, well-educated college graduates. Among them, Dean Muncaster, who came second in his class at Western, was a leading light.

Dean's thesis at Western was on Canadian Tire. A.J. Billes had no sooner read it than he recruited its author. When Muncaster reported for work in 1957, he was almost the very first employee of the company to hold a university degree.

One of Dean's first jobs was in dealer relations, where he undertook to study, in painstaking detail, the differences between stores that performed well and those that didn't. Such comparisons were nothing new, of course. But in the past they had been mostly limited to sales and profits. Dean compared inventory turns, sales per square foot and sales per employee and more. Such measurements would become standard yardsticks for evaluating

Owning a Car
in the Sixties

During the turbulent late sixties, motorists used their cars to express not only their economic status, but their political and social beliefs as well. The big-finned classics of the early sixties (*right*) were soon challenged by the emergence of more compact and economical foreign automobiles. Whatever one drove, Canadian Tire could still provide all the auto accessories (*bottom right*).

ord it? price the Newport!

The beautiful surprise from Chrysler. Proof that Chrysler's still in building them full-size only. No jr. editions! And what do you rice? A new Firebolt V-8 delivered 510 miles on a tankful Oil supervised test. Torsion-bar suspension, perennial perts. Unibody—one-piece welded, specially padded dipped in seven different baths to prevent rust. And lternator that produces electric current even at en-y Newport. Then get set for a surprise at the price.
■ WINDSOR ■ NEW YORKER ■ 300/G

Chrysler '61

featuring the NEWPORT
—a full-size Chrysler in a new, lower price range

In the heady days of the late 1960s, Canadians hit the road. A Volkswagen "beetle" was one of the most popular cars of the time, especially when decorated with stick-on flowers or bumper stickers (above) announcing the places to see — and be seen.

CUSTOM-FIT
...for new car elegance

Smart, Practical and Low-Priced! **16.99** SET

Cool, woven polypropylene covers in handsome, subdued patterns to complement all car interiors. Virtually stainproof, spills and soil wipe off easily with a damp cloth! With leatherette trim along bolster, seat edge, back of front seat, gusset and skirting; harmonizing welting. Available for most popular car models, including compacts. Colors: Blue, Green, Red, Brown.
52-F—Complete set; front and rear 16.99
52-FO—Cover for front seat only 10.25

WHEN ORDERING: Give full details of car and covers required.

Popular De Luxe 'Puff-Saran' Covers **25.49** SET

retailing excellence in the years ahead but at the time they were still uncommon. A.J. was impressed with young Muncaster's work. Three years later, at the age of twenty-seven, he was named to the company's Board of Directors.

By 1966, when Dean Muncaster became president, Canadian Tire had grown too large — and too complicated — to be governed by one person. Muncaster needed a management team. He appointed vice-presidents of marketing, distribution and merchandising and, within very clearly defined areas, gave them broad authority. Dubbed "The Great Quarterback," he explains his thinking: "If one is going to aspire to run a large organization, then one has to invest a lot of control and responsibility in certain people.... I had kind of assimilated the fact that a lot of successful companies were operating that way." Years later, the management system he employed would be termed "loose-tight." At one point, the prestigious U.S. consulting firm McKinsey & Co. named Dean Muncaster "loose-tight's" number-one all-time practitioner.

Other innovations followed. The company's cumbersome distribution system was rebuilt. The word "warehouse," with its connotations of goods — and money — gathering dust on the shelf, was banished. Better to *distribute* products, to speed them from factory to checkout counter, and so a twenty-three million-dollar mechanized distribution centre was built in Brampton, northwest of Toronto. Canadian Tire assembled a fleet of one hundred diesel rigs and six hundred trailers, every last one of them emblazoned with the red triangle. And to give the transports even greater promotional mileage, Canadian Tire took a cue from Labatt's and washed them before every major trip.

Of course, moving products was only half the battle. The real trick was to carry as little merchandise as possible without ever having to apologize to the customers for being out of stock. That's where computers came in. In the late 1950s, few corporations were using them, and even fewer retailers. Canadian Tire was a pioneer. Their first computer — a colossal,

Dean Muncaster, president of Canadian Tire from 1966 to 1985, pioneered the management system that would see the store through years of enormous growth and change.

Masterc[raft] Scrubbable Vinyl Wall Coverings

Pre-Pasted, just immerse in water, apply and smooth with wet sponge. **Dry-Strippable**, peels off easily, won't damage walls when removed.

Low, low price **3.69** Single roll

SOLD IN DOUBLE ROLLS ONLY. Single roll prices let you compare, double rolls save you money — doubles produce five 8-ft. strips with 2 ft. left for matching; singles produce two 8-ft. strips with 5 ft. left.

When wallpaper has this much going for it, you would expect to pay more. But not when you shop Canadian Tire. And you choose from exclusive patterns that you won't find anywhere else. Our designs are elegant enough for the most glamorous room setting, yet tough enough to be 'kid-proof' anywhere in the house. Pick bold florals, smart stripes, classic gold-traced formals, textured effects and warm colonials. Soil and grease-resistant, wipe clean with a damp cloth. Sold in double rolls only to cover about 64 sq. ft.
68-9500X—Note the low price. Single roll. . . . 3.69

WATER TROUGH
Sturdy cardboard. Moisture-proof, folds flat for storage. **43c**
68-9599—Reusable

Only a few patterns are shown above . . . See the complete line at your local Canadian Tire store.

Mactac Covering
44 patterns in easy-on 18-in. decorator vinyl. 6' roll **1.39** ea.

Walls, furniture even ornaments come alive with this practical vinyl cover-up. Just cut to fit, peel off the backing and apply. Wipes clean with a damp cloth. Available in choice of 44 patterns from popular woodgrains to colorful florals.
49-9005X—6-ft. roll, 18" wide. Only 1.39
If you require a smaller quantity, buy only what you need, 18" wide. Per running yard . . . . . . .7[ ]

Flower Power

Suburban families seeking the latest in home decor needed to look no farther than the 1974 Canadian Tire catalogue (*above right*) for inspiration. Unadorned walls in the rec room (*top*) or bedroom (*above*) could quickly be transformed with stylish vinyl or Mactac covering. Children could choose from lunchboxes featuring Barbie (*left*), a floral explosion (*centre*), or the "Sock it to me" slogan.

14

15

16

CANADIAN TIRE CENTENNIAL TOUR

In 1967, Canada turned one hundred. Canadians from coast to coast, in towns big and small, marked the event. The biggest celebration was Montreal's Expo '67, the spectacular world's fair held on a series of islands built in the St. Lawrence River. Citizens were encouraged to come up with their own Centennial projects, and Canadian Tire got into the swing of things by organizing the Centennial Car Rally, a parade of vintage automobiles that motored through Canadian towns and cities before winding up at Expo '67.

CANADIAN TIRE

SPRING & SUMMER 1967
The Canadian's Complete Automotive, Hardware, and Sporting Goods Store

1867·1967 On July 24th, one hundred magnificent Classic and Antique cars, some of them 50 years old or more, will set out for "Expo" from several different places across Canada. Stop-overs and side events en route will enable you and thousands of Canadians to see these historic vehicles at close quarters. Awards will be made for performance, elegance, authenticity, etc., with a grand finale starting at "Expo" on August 3rd. This is the CANADIAN TIRE CENTENNIAL TOUR . . . a salute to our country in her 100th year!

Index on Pages 141-142

SI VOUS PARLEZ FRANÇAIS, VOYEZ PAGE 130

Crowds in the millions flocked to see Canada's $1 billion birthday extravaganza. Popular destinations at the fair included (top) the United States pavilion, a geodesic dome designed by Buckminster Fuller; (left) the inverted pyramid marking Canada's national pavilion; and (bottom) the "broken pillar" on the right that topped the British pavilion. (Right) Even in the midst of such feverish modernity, a symbol of an older more placid Canada, a Mountie on horseback, could still be found.

CYCLO-MAGIE
COUGAR
SUPER CYCLE

Bleu argent
pour FILLE
48.88

48.88
Bleu argent
pour GARÇON

COUGAR
X-100
de GARÇON
57.77

CANADIAN TIRE CORPORATION LTD., 837-857 YONGE ST., TORONTO, ONTARIO

97

FOR A SUPER RIDE...
Ride
SUPER-CYCLE

Boys' and Girls' Sizes
36.95

① STANDARD SUPER-CYCLE
Men's & Ladies' Sizes . . . 37.95
Junior, Juvenile Sizes . . . 35.95

44.95

② DE LUXE SUPER-CYCLE
Compares With Models Costing As Much As 61.50

35.95
③ SIDEWALK SUPER-CYCLE
For The 5 to 8-Year Olds

USE YOUR CREDIT
Shopping is Easier With Our
New Credit Plan—See Page 5
DOWN PAYMENTS AS LOW AS 5.00

A shiny new bicycle was every child's dream. The sporty Super-Cycle, seen above on a 1960 catalogue page, gave way to the beloved banana-seat by 1968 (above left). It was always possible to customize your bike by picking out new tires or saddles (right). Later, biking would become a popular adult pastime as well (left).

⑦ ⑥

tube-filled IBM 650 RAMAC — filled an air-conditioned room and had all of sixty-four kilobytes of memory. As computers grew faster and smaller, Canadian Tire kept pace, buying the latest machines for inventory management. The company grew so deft with the new technology that in the late 1960s, IBM chose Canadian Tire to test its state-of-the-art IMPACT program. IMPACT was designed to predict how much stock the retailer would need based on sales, purchasing lead times and other factors. "It was the first attempt to do that on a computerized basis and they thought we had the best appreciation of inventory management," says Muncaster.

Other major changes accompanied Canadian Tire's entry into the digital age. By 1970, Canadian Tire was the single largest retail advertiser in Canada. Full-page newspaper advertisements became common, and once each month daily newspapers across Canada carried a promotional flyer. And the catalogue now consistently exceeded two hundred pages. Company revenues skyrocketed, rising

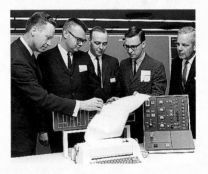

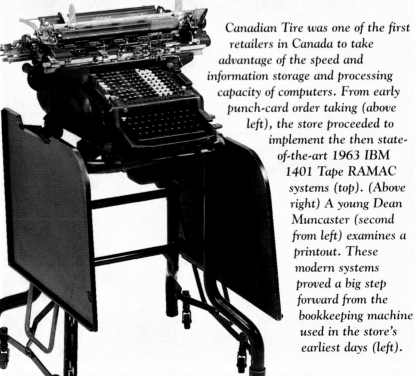

Canadian Tire was one of the first retailers in Canada to take advantage of the speed and information storage and processing capacity of computers. From early punch-card order taking (above left), the store proceeded to implement the then state-of-the-art 1963 IBM 1401 Tape RAMAC systems (top). (Above right) A young Dean Muncaster (second from left) examines a printout. These modern systems proved a big step forward from the bookkeeping machine used in the store's earliest days (left).

During the sixties and seventies Canadian Tire continued to expand across the nation. (Top left) A ribbon-cutting in La Sarre, Quebec, 1972; (top right) inside the Woodstock, New Brunswick, store, 1969; (above right) "Giddy-up, shoppers!" Cashiers make like cowboys in Brandon, Manitoba, 1973; (above left) standing on guard at the auto parts department, Corner Brook, Newfoundland, 1969; (below) grand opening at the St. Vital, Manitoba, store in 1968.

from just under $100 million when Muncaster was made president in 1966 to $683 million in 1976, an average increase of twenty percent a year.

Under Dean Muncaster, Canadian Tire spread nationwide. In 1966, Canadian Tire opened its first store west of the Ontario border, in Winnipeg. By 1980 they had made it all the way to British Columbia. The total number of stores mushroomed from about 225 to 333. Store sizes grew as well. In 1953, Walter Muncaster's twelve-thousand-square-foot store was the largest in the chain. Under his son's rule, old stores were replaced by much larger ones, some even double the size of Walter's. Attention was lavished on the science of store design — sight lines, merchandisers, product placement, shelf height, signage and colour. And the changes didn't stop there. In 1969, more than half of Canadian Tire's shipments to dealers were automotive parts and accessories. Just seven years later, two-thirds of them comprised household, hardware and leisure products. Perhaps as a result, many more women were now shopping at Canadian Tire.

Since the day when the first Associate Store opened, Canadian Tire's dealers have played a key role in the company's success. The 1960s saw a new breed of dealer, managers who were in many ways similar to the executives who were transforming home office and, in fact, some of them came from IBM. Whatever their origins, they would transform "Dealerland," as it was known.

One of the boldest among them was A. J. D. "Arch" Brown, with his huge and hugely successful Barrie, Ontario, store. Prior to joining Canadian Tire, Arch was the youngest district sales manager in the history of General Motors in Canada, a record that still stands to this day. But he observed that many older GM executives seemed to be barely hanging on to their jobs. In the independent spirit of the Canadian Tire

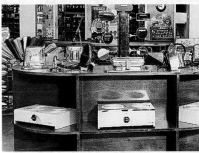

An increase in the number of household and leisure products available (above) brought more female customers into the stores. Now, as well as fishing rods and monkey wrenches, the 1965 catalogue, shown below, offered everything for the fashionably coiffed woman.

The Happy Life of An Advertising Mascot

He was never given a name. But for almost thirty years the old gent with the white hair and mustache was a popular advertising symbol for Canadian Tire. The catalogue covers at right show highlights from his career and how his image was adapted to changing times.

He made his debut in the spring of 1941 and at first was mainly a figure of fun, boasting about his fishing prowess or caught dozing by two younger men in uniform, presumably his sons. In the postwar period a curvaceous blonde enters the picture and throughout the fifties the covers take a mildly naughty turn with the old man being continually diverted by a statuesque "dame," often to the chagrin of his sons. By the 1960s, the covers reflect more wholesome family scenes although the old man still seems to have a twinkle for the fetching blonde even while she is pressing him into service with household chores as the two sons make their escape. By the late 1960s the old man is clearly on the way out and only head shots of the four characters appear along with merchandise on the cover of the Spring/Summer 1968/9 catalogue. By 1970 merchandise alone remains. Although perhaps inappropriate for modern tastes and sensibilities, the old man, the blonde and the two sons are a reminder of a time when familiar characters and whimsical "story" covers could be a part of successful advertising.

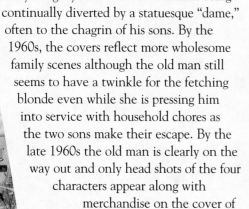

Dealer associations help fellow Associate Dealers keep in touch. (Top) Quebec dealers pose for a group shot. (Above) Northern dealers assemble at the 1963 annual convention. Arch Brown (right) was one of the new breed of dealers, as active in increasing sales as he was in community service.

dealer, Arch resolved that his livelihood would never be dependent on the caprice of an employer. He contacted his high-school chum Dick Billes, J.W.'s son, who was by the late 1950s a senior executive at Canadian Tire. He wanted a store, but lacked the money. And so a deal was made: if Arch worked five years at home office, the company would lend him the money he needed.

In 1963, Arch took over the Barrie dealership, one he knew to be an under-performer, ripe with potential. The store itself was twenty thousand square feet in area and situated downtown. He dismissed the entire staff and hired all but a few of them back at a fifty-percent-higher wage. He splurged on advertising and promotion, embraced the computer age and carefully managed his inventory. Sometimes on Saturdays he would do a little market research while standing guard in the parking lot to make sure only *his* customers used the spaces. As customers left, he asked every one whether they found what they were looking for.

The store was busy and profitable. But that wasn't good enough. When a three-storey fifty-thousand-square-foot building on the outskirts of Barrie became available, he jumped at it. It was an enormous gamble. Even though other huge new stores were opening across the country, there was nothing to compare with it. Some dubbed it Brown's Folly, and for the first year it looked as if they might be right. He lost a lot of money, but the decision to move to the suburbs proved to be the right one. Between 1963 and 1995, when he retired, sales at Brown's store increased eighty-fold.

His success was due in no small measure to his extraordinary community involvement. Over the years Arch Brown has chaired, served, sat on, endowed or in some way participated in just about every arts, charitable and educational institution in Barrie: Junior Achievement, Rotary Club, Georgian College, Canadian Tire Child Protection Foundation — the list is endless. For his services, Arch has been given the Order of Canada. Among the many Canadian Tire dealers who make a point of putting something back into their communities, Arch Brown is just one of many shining examples.

In 1980, Arch was part of a network of 327 dealers in the Canadian Tire organization. Company sales had topped one billion dollars for the first time. The vibrant family-run enterprise that J.W. Billes had left behind twenty-four years earlier was now a modern corporation — professionally managed and fully computerized. And what better symbol of that change could there be than the decision in 1978 to move the home office from the cramped confines above the flagship store at 837 Yonge Street to a glass-and-steel office tower farther north at 2180 Yonge Street?

In many more ways than one, Canadian Tire was moving farther along the road.

By 1980 a fleet of distinctive red and white Canadian Tire rigs regularly crossed the country, moving goods — and acting as rolling advertisements.

Canadian Tire and Hockey

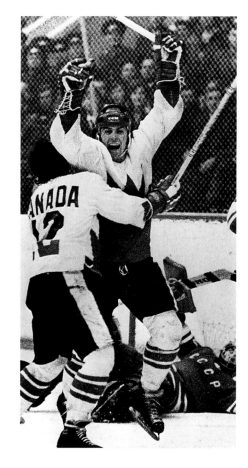

It's the Canadian dream. You're in the third period of the seventh game of a tightly fought Stanley Cup series. With just seconds left on the clock, you shoot. You score, the buzzer goes and the Leafs — or the Oilers or the Canadiens — are victorious.

For a child, making that dream come true means hours spent practising, honing your skating or stick-handling. For a parent, it means getting up long before the winter sun has risen. It means shivering in an echoing arena, with only a foam cup filled with coffee to warm you, the frosty air punctuated by the bang of a puck on boards, the shriek of a whistle, the excited cries of a dozen eager young voices.

Canadian Tire is a part of the dream, too. Today, the store is the largest retail supplier of the skates, the helmets and the sticks young players need — in fact, Canadian Tire is the nation's largest supplier of every kind of hockey equipment. And the company's involvement doesn't end there. Throughout the country, in small towns and big cities, many Associate Stores sponsor local teams, helping countless Canadian boys — and more and more Canadian girls — to realize their dreams of glory in Canada's national pastime.

Making a dream like Paul Henderson's (above left) come true, means starting early (left). Canadian Tire's commitment to amateur hockey has included both providing the equipment (right) and sponsoring the teams (above).

It Happened in the Sixties and Seventies

For Canadians in every region, this was a period of contrast and contradiction. National pride and confidence reached new heights, finding fervent expression in a one-billion-dollar celebration of the country's one hundredth birthday called Expo'67. More than fifty million people came to Montreal to see it. Patriotic spirit was expressed, too, in the rock-star status accorded a charismatic new prime minister by the name of Pierre Elliott Trudeau.

(Top) Pierre Trudeau's appeal extended well beyond the polls through the sixties and seventies. (Above right) Canada's athletes enter Montreal's Olympic Stadium (above) during the opening ceremonies of the 1976 Summer Games. (Right) The record-breaking CN Tower was constructed in Toronto in 1975.

Also during the sixties and seventies:

• Canada made a significant contribution to the blossoming folk and rock genres of the 1960s with songwriters and performers such as Leonard Cohen, Gordon Lightfoot, Ian & Sylvia, the Guess Who, Joni Mitchell, Robbie Robertson and Neil Young. Gilles Vigneault penned "Mon Pays," a song that became Quebec's unofficial anthem. In the 1970s the trend continued with Rush, Heart and Dan Hill topping the charts in English Canada and René Simard and Harmonium big among francophones.

All in all, Canada had never felt better about itself.

Meanwhile, however, an opposing nationalism began to flourish in Quebec. The Quiet Revolution, in which Quebec began flexing its political muscle, was followed by the birth of the Parti Québécois. Under René Lévesque, the new party was elected to run the province in 1976. Four years later the first referendum on sovereignty was held.

Strong growth in employment and a rising standard of living marked the 1960s. In the following decade this gave way to slower growth, inflation, labour strife and eco-nomic uncertainty. Canadians came to realize that their fantastic postwar prosperity was not to be taken for granted in the 1970s.

In federal politics, the challenge of governing in a recession proved too much for John Diefenbaker's Conservatives, who were re-elected in 1962 as a minority government. A short time later, the Liberals came to power, also as a minority, under career diplomat Lester B. Pearson. Pierre Trudeau would succeed him in 1968 and go on to become one of the longest-serving prime ministers in Canadian history.

• In sports, Canadians were glued to their television sets through most of September 1972 as the best hockey players from Canada and the Soviet Union locked sticks for the "Summit on Ice" series. An astounding twelve and a half million Canadians watched Paul Henderson score the goal that won Canada the series in game eight. On April 12, 1980, in St. John's, Terry Fox dipped his artificial leg in the ocean and set out for Victoria on the Marathon of Hope, a drive to raise money for cancer research.

• Three Canadians invented the IMAX film and projection system for use at the Canadian pavilion at Expo 1970 in Osaka, Japan. In 1975, the CN Tower, the tallest freestanding structure in the world at 1,815 feet, was completed in Toronto. And in 1979, Canadians Chris Haney and Scott Abbott invented Trivial Pursuit, one of the most successful board games in history.

Always in touch with the times, a 1965 Canadian Tire catalogue cover (right)

CANADIAN TIRE CORP'N.
SPRING & SUMMER 1965

A GOOD CHOICE!

continued to be topical through the national flag debate of the mid-1960s (above).

Canadian Tire Today
1981~1997

CHAPTER FIVE

Canadian Tire Today

1981 ~ 1997

THE SCENE OPENS ON A PERFECT WINTER'S DAY — crisp, cold and clear. A group of boys in skates stands on a frozen pond.

"I'll take Joe," calls one.

"I want Steve," shouts another, beckoning.

"Tommy, Mike, Patrick, come on," says the first.

Finally, one freckle-faced boy, the youngest of the bunch, stands alone.

"I guess that leaves Albert," says one of the boys who have been doing the picking.

"Hey," says his opposite, with that special brand of callousness that only kids seem able to muster, "He's your kid brother. *You* take him."

We all know the feeling, but Albert's tale doesn't end here. After a quick tour of the Canadian Tire hockey department, we pick up the thread of the story a dozen or so years later at what we presume is an NHL game. There's an arena stuffed with frenzied fans. They're going wild. "Albert! ... Albert! ... Albert! ... Albert!" they chant as the man himself steps onto the ice. And to close, the head coach of the other

team says simply, "I sure wish we had a guy like Albert."

When it premiered in 1983, the "Albert" television commercial, as it came to be known, spoke directly to the hopes and dreams of every kid and grown-up kid in the country. So popular was the spot that, for a time, hockey fans across the country would chant "Albert" whenever their team was behind. It was the first of several commercials — all conceived by W.B. Doner & Co., the retailer's advertising agency since 1981 — that explored the special connection between Canadian Tire and its customers. "Bike Story," another huge hit, was first aired in 1988. It tells the story of a farmer's son, who "slept, ate, lived and breathed" the bike he'd cut out from the Canadian Tire catalogue and whose father, touchingly, surprises him with it in the end.

By the 1980s, Canadian Tire had earned more than a marketing niche, it had gained a place in the Canadian psyche. But this wasn't really surprising. Canadian Tire had flourished in Canada by moulding itself to the psychology, buying habits, and preferences of Canadians.

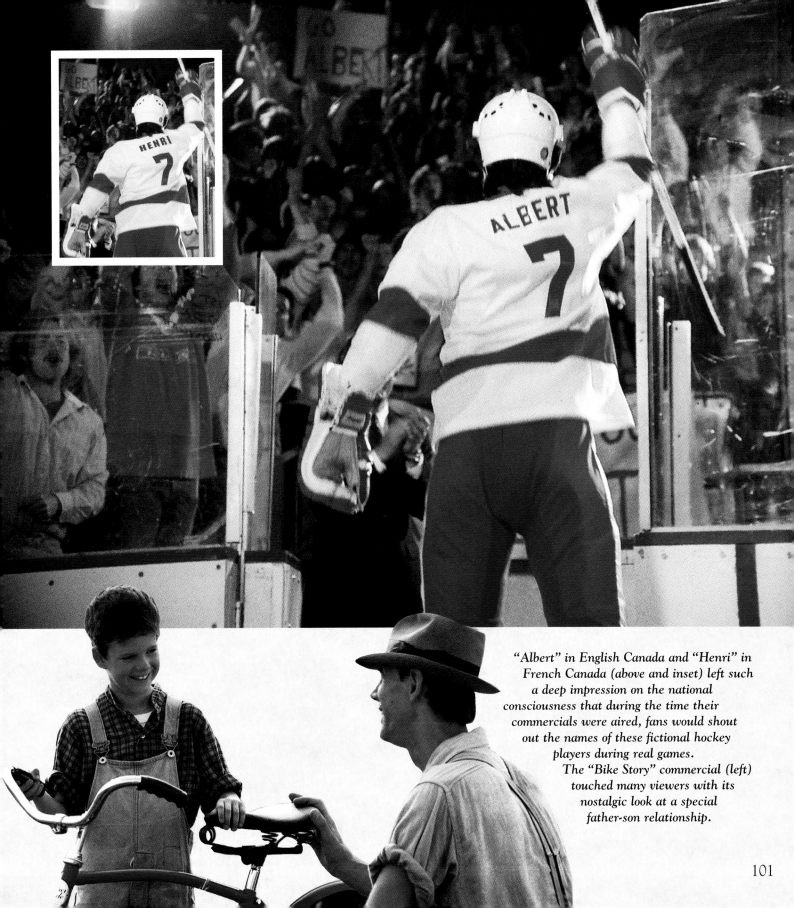

"Albert" in English Canada and "Henri" in French Canada (above and inset) left such a deep impression on the national consciousness that during the time their commercials were aired, fans would shout out the names of these fictional hockey players during real games.

The "Bike Story" commercial (left) touched many viewers with its nostalgic look at a special father-son relationship.

(Above) Martha Billes, daughter of A.J. and one of the company's principal shareholders. (Below) Dean Groussman, company president from 1985 to 1992. (Opposite) Today the company is led by Stephen Bachand, whose many innovations will take Canadian Tire into the next century.

So the company could be forgiven for basking in a sepia glow. By 1990, sales had hit a record $3 billion. Net income, at $144 million, was the second-highest ever. As well, the thorny question of Canadian Tire's long-term ownership was settled once and for all. Since J.W.'s death in 1956, none of his or A.J.'s descendants ever individually had a large enough piece of the company on their own to take control. But in the early 1980s, A.J.'s three children collectively assumed a majority position and, after nearly selling their interest in 1987, they have held it ever since. Martha, a Calgary-based independent business woman, Fred, a former dealer, and David, a car-racing enthusiast, who spent most of his engineering career developing high-performance engines, each hold just over twenty percent of the retailer's all-important voting shares. Collectively, the dealers hold a similar amount. Then, the corporation's deferred profit-sharing plan owns 12.2 percent of the remaining voting shares. The non-voting shares are widely held by the general public.

But in the 1990s, retailing in this country went through the wringer, buffeted by recession and the rapidly changing preferences of increasingly demanding, better-educated consumers. Early in the decade, the company's managers — headed by Dean Groussman (president from 1985 to 1992) — were under no illusions about the threat represented by a possible retail invasion from the south. In the company's 1991 annual report, Groussman predicted that, thanks to the Canada/U.S. Free Trade Agreement coming into effect the previous year, the company could expect some strong competition from American retailers in the years ahead.

Stephen E. Bachand, who took over as president in 1993, was hired to lead the company against this competition. Every aspect of the business was scrutinized for cost reductions. "By the time the U.S. retailers started arriving, Canadian Tire had made a very large number of the adjustments they needed to make," says veteran merchandising analyst David Brodie of CIBC Wood Gundy Securities Inc.

To prepare for this new challenge, Canadian Tire returned to its roots — to focus on

customers and what they wanted. The greatest changes came in store format. Some Canadian Tire stores had suffered from their own success. The vast range of products offered, the great prices and convenient locations all translated into more customers than the old-format stores could comfortably handle. The result: occasional congestion, crowding and line-ups at the cashiers.

Responding to the company's customers, the company and its Associate Dealers continued to improve by developing a completely new design for many Canadian Tire stores. In their quest, planners laboured over one full-scale mock-up after another. They looked at different exterior store colours, designs and entrances; they evaluated various shelf heights, lighting types, aisle locations, sign styles and hues. They were looking for the design that would see Canadian Tire into the twenty-first century.

The improvements in the new stores are myriad. First, they're bigger. There are now four standard store sizes, with the largest being fifty-three-thousand square feet. More space means more products in every department. It also means dealers can take those oil filters, screwdrivers and lawn tractors out of the back storage room and put them in the store where more customers can see them. With more goods on the shelves, staff spend less time restocking and more time assisting customers.

To help customers find their way around, the stores' main departments have been colour-coded: red for automotive, blue for home products, green for sports and leisure. The shelves at the front of the store are lower than at the back, so that customers have an unobstructed view of each department from the instant they enter the building. For good measure, the planners have put a store map and information kiosk near the entrance. The aisles are wide and clearly labeled with triangular signs. Gone is the glare of the old, flickering fluorescent lights; new stores are bathed in the cool, even glow of metal halide. Additional vertical signs and shelf maps clearly point the way, so that even people looking for small loose items — say a single 3/8" screw — can put their hands on them.

The new store format (opposite) makes it even easier for customers to locate products and services. Canadian Tire's popular Christmas campaign features Santa and Scrooge in English-speaking Canada (below) and Michel Forget and Gratteux in Quebec (above).

Anyone who still needs help can press one of the many customer-service buttons strategically located throughout the store or use a touch-screen kiosk. There are also bar-code readers handy so customer can verify the price of products themselves.

Stephen Bachand has pushed the new store format hard. The company is implementing a $1-billion capital expenditures program, one that will see over 250 stores renovated, relocated, rebuilt or redesigned by the year 2000. It's the single largest capital program ever undertaken by Canadian Tire. But Bachand emphasizes that there's no such thing as the perfect store. The new format is a starting point, nothing more. Every year, in hundreds of subtle ways, the format undergoes constant refinement to lead the competition. An entrance leading directly to the automotive-parts counter, for example, was added in 1995. "You've got to be fleet of foot," he told one reporter in 1995. "I'm never, ever satisfied."

Dealers are excited by the new format for one simple reason: it works. Claude L'Heureux's store in Cowansville, Quebec, was the first to undergo the metamorphosis. Since then, the number of customers the other new-format stores welcome has increased by twenty percent. The amount a customer spends in a store visit has also jumped twenty percent and sales are up by fifty percent year over year overall.

The new store format, the overhaul of the distribution system, the new customer service policies: these and many other changes championed by Bachand, the CTC management and the Associate Dealers are centrepieces of what he's dubbed the "New Tire," a catch phrase that was even

emblazoned on the cover of the company's 1995 annual report.

Shortly after the U.S./Canada Free Trade Agreement was implemented eight years ago, as Canadian retailers waited anxiously for the giants of American retailing to march on Canada, there were many in the business community who believed that Canadian Tire would be among the early casualties. But thanks to sound management, the strength of the dealer system and the dedication and perseverance of Canadian Tire employees, that prediction could not have been further from the truth.

In 1997, Canadian Tire enjoys strong sales and, with the solid investments being made, excellent prospects. Those who feared that the company might be forced to close its doors were dead wrong. As Stephen Bachand told employees in the president's annual State of the Tire address, "We're busy building new doors to new stores right across the country."

(Above) Canadian Tire's state-of-the-art distribution centre. (Below) At the new-format stores changes are not restricted to just the inside, as this exterior shot shows.

It happened in the Eighties and Nineties

Politically and economically, this was a roller coaster time, a midway ride that most of us would have probably declined to board, had we any sense of what was in store — and had we any choice.

For many Canadians, though not all, the 1980s represented one of the greatest periods of economic expansion in the country's history. In many parts of the country, affluence was in conspicuous evidence. Real estate prices in Toronto and Vancouver soared, unemployment in many regions fell, and money seemed to flow like wine. Some of the beneficiaries of this prosperity were members of the baby-boom generation, and a new word was coined to described these young, urban professionals: they were dubbed "Yuppies." Wrapped warmly

Also during the eighties and nineties:

• The Walt Disney Company announced in November 1995 a decision to open animation studios in Vancouver and Toronto, furnishing tangible proof — if any was needed — that Canada was becoming the Hollywood of the animation business. One industry leader referred to Toronto's Sheridan College as the "Harvard of animation schools." Quebecois comedian André-Philippe Gagnon becomes a hit — in two languages — with his pop star impersonations. In 1994, a little-known Canadian comedian, Jim Carrey, joined the firmament of Hollywood superstars with three films: *The Mask, Dumb and Dumber,* and *Ace Ventura, Pet Detective.*

• Anne of Green Gables (the character created by Canadian writer Lucy Maude Montgomery and brought to life in a successful Canadian television series) was so popular in Japan that by 1995 travel agencies were booking ten thousand package trips to Prince Edward Island each year.

in an economic security blanket, many Canadians turned their attention and passion to saving the planet.

And then came the big correction. In 1989 and 1990, the Canadian economy followed its neighbour to the south into a rapid tailspin. It was to be the worst recession since the 1930s. Even when the economists told us in the early 1990s that the "recovery" had come, unemployment levels remained so high that nobody believed them.

Meanwhile, provincial and federal politicians led by Conservative Prime Minister Brian Mulroney tried vainly to hammer out a consensus that would bring Quebec — the only province not to sign the patriated constitution in 1982 — back into the fold. The Meech Lake Accord, the Charlottetown Accord, all other efforts to date — closed-door or open-door — have not yet succeeded.

In the early 1990s the accumulated debt at all levels of government actually exceeded the size of the economy itself. With strong public backing, Premier Ralph Klein in Alberta and the once-profligate Liberals in Ottawa took an axe to their budgets. Most of the provinces followed suit. Canada's provincial and federal governments were retreating to pre-war levels of economic involvement. It was their ardent desire that Canada's economic fate be placed in the hands of the private sector. By 1997, the debt-rating agencies had pulled down the red flags, consumer spending was gradually improving, and exports were increasing.

• Quebec director Denys Arcand garners international acclaim for *The Decline of the American Empire* and *Jesus of Montreal*.

• One of the most successful comedy shows in Canadian history, *This Hour Has Twenty-Two Minutes*, was launched in 1993. Two years later, the curtain fell on *Front Page Challenge* after thirty-eight years on the air. In the mid-1990s, Canada was the second-largest creator and exporter of children's television in the world.

• During the 1990s, with performers such as k.d. lang, Daniel Lanois, the Tragically Hip, Rita MacNeil, and the dazzling Mitsou, Canadian music exports were never stronger. In 1996, country singer/songwriter Shania Twain and her pop compatriots Céline Dion and Alanis Morissette formed the Canadian juggernaut that dominated the Grammy Awards in the United States.

• Wayne Gretzky rose to become one of the two or three best hockey players of all time, leading the Edmonton Oilers to Stanley Cup wins in 1985, 1988 and 1990.

(Far left) An unemployed man advertising for work in Halifax. (Middle left) Terry Fox running in the Marathon of Hope. (Near left) Chanteuse Céline Dion winning big at the Grammys and (right) Wayne Gretzky leading the Oilers to victory.

Epilogue

Epilogue

VISIT THE EXECUTIVE OFFICES OF CANADIAN TIRE Corporation, Limited in Toronto and one of the first things you'll notice is the Wall of Winners. Stretching from floor to ceiling and running some fifty feet along a hallway, it consists of countless framed letters from customers who have taken the time to write and commend the actions of a cashier, a dealer, a customer rep or some other remarkable employee at their local Canadian Tire store. Scan the wall and you'll discover Tilbury, Ontario, dealer Denis Léger, who put up two families overnight in his store when they were stranded by a snowstorm. Or Karen Decruiter, a customer-service representative, who took the time to find a local dog breeder for the couple who were reminded of the dog they had just lost by one in a Canadian Tire commercial. And you'll read about Paula Zinck in Bridgewater, Nova Scotia, who spent several days meticulously researching and recording item numbers and

prices so a customer whose barn and workshop had burnt down could replace his lost tools as quickly as possible.

The Wall of Winners is President and CEO Stephen Bachand's way of honouring good deeds at Canadian Tire, of paying tribute to acts of kindness that benefit customers, dealers, employees and the Corporation alike. But it's also a means of keeping alive the flame of dedicated service that was first lit back on September 15, 1922, and fed, tended and stoked by thousands of employees and dealers since that time. It is perfectly embodied in Myrel Pardoe, who celebrated sixty-five years as a Canadian Tire employee last April first.

Much of the credit for Canadian Tire's success has to go to its employees. Call it enfranchisement, empowerment, or simply caring, they have always struggled to do their best for the company and its customers. Leadership, too, has played a key role. J.W. Billes had the good sense and the good fortune to catch not one, but two, rising stars: the

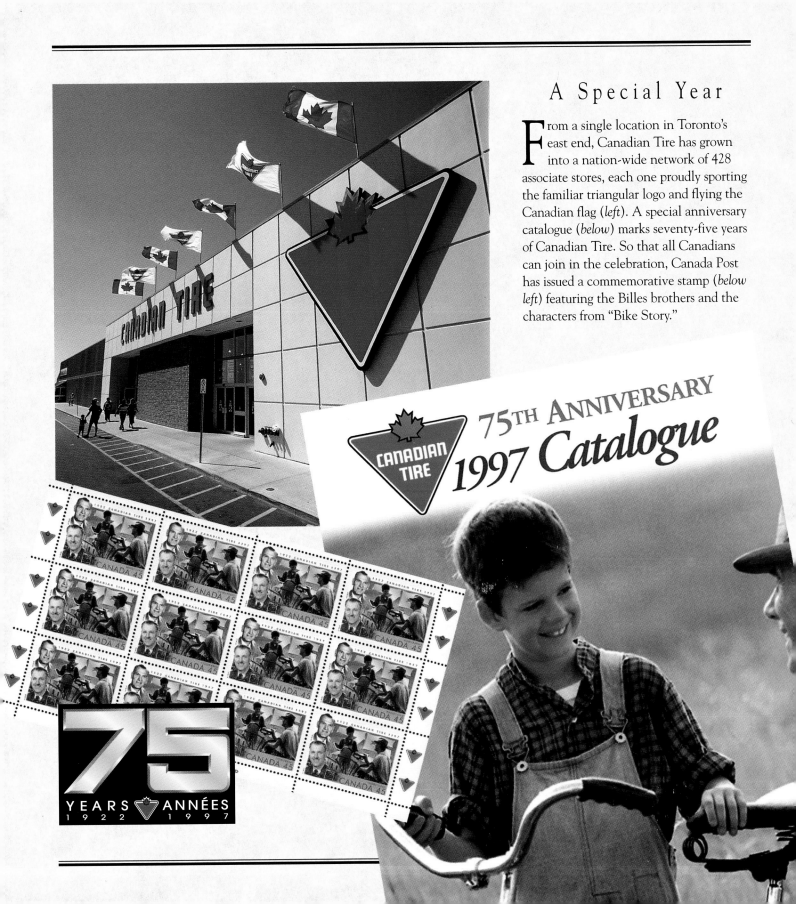

A Special Year

From a single location in Toronto's east end, Canadian Tire has grown into a nation-wide network of 428 associate stores, each one proudly sporting the familiar triangular logo and flying the Canadian flag (*left*). A special anniversary catalogue (*below*) marks seventy-five years of Canadian Tire. So that all Canadians can join in the celebration, Canada Post has issued a commemorative stamp (*below left*) featuring the Billes brothers and the characters from "Bike Story."

automobile and retailing, and he made the most of them both. He developed the idea of the Associate Stores, believing that if you give people control over their material future they will work harder. The popularity of franchising among retailers today shows just how right he was. At a time when few other retailers had house brands, he and A.J. were creating and promoting them tirelessly.

Strength followed strength as A.J. Billes took over the presidency in 1956 and launched a series of bold initiatives that included that stroke of marketing genius, Canadian Tire 'Money.' A.J. also took on the oil companies and made Canadian Tire the largest independent gas retailer in the country. Following him, Dean Muncaster used the principles of scientific management to turn the company into a fullfledged modern corporation while overseeing a bold expansion program that took Canadian Tire to the shores of the Pacific. Dean Groussman helped steer the company through the economically difficult late eighties and early nineties. And in recent years, Stephen Bachand, in defending the retailer's turf against an invasion from the south, has built a better, stronger Canadian Tire in the process.

Over the years, as Canadians changed, Canadian Tire changed with them. In 1922, the vast majority of people had little money to spare despite six long days of work each week. And Canadian Tire's first slogan, We'll Make Your Dollars Go Farther, spoke to that. As each passing decade brought more leisure time and disposable income, Canadian Tire offered an ever broader range of products. Today we renovate our homes, hop into our cars and escape to the cottage, shoot hoops, play tennis, plant a shrub, or just water the lawn — all with Canadian Tire's help.

Great employees, strong leadership, retail innovation, and an unerring ability to anticipate changes in customers' needs and values have all given rise to a corporation that today sells more than 68,000 different products through 428 stores across Canada.

But Canadian Tire in the 1990s is more than just a successful company. It is also a good corporate citizen. The Canadian Tire Child Protection Foundation was launched in

The Canadian Tire Child Protection Foundation (top centre), created in 1993, supports charities whose mandates focus on child protection. The Cycle Safe® Program promotes bicycle safety and helmet awareness with materials like the "Gearing Up" video (middle centre). AquaQuest™ is the safety program of the Canadian Red Cross (bottom centre).

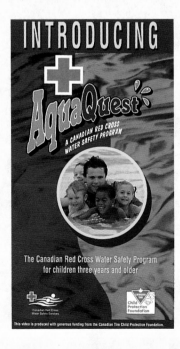

Canadian Tire and Community Service

Canadian Tire has a long history of community service and corporate sponsorship. The company has participated in the Tour de L'ile de Montreal bike rally (*below*) as well as in amateur hockey across the country (*far left*).

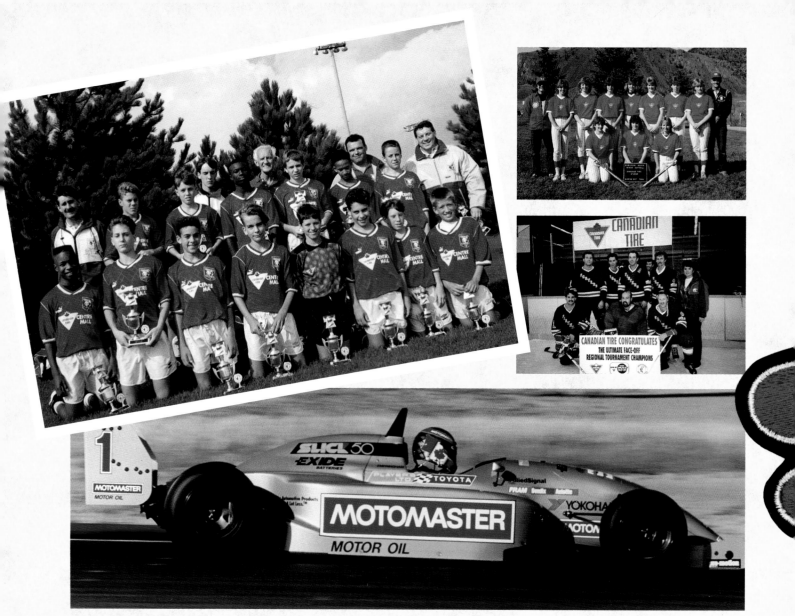

Canadian Tire's community involvement and corporate sponsorship spans the country. (Top left) a soccer team sponsored by Hamilton, Ontario's Centre Mall store; (top right) a softball team in Kamloops, B.C.; (second from top right) sponsoring the Ultimate Face-Off;

(centre) the company sponsors both Formula Atlantic and Indy Light class race cars; (bottom left) promoting the Streetball challenge; (bottom right) a bicycle donation to the Ontario Provincial Police Patrol at Turkey Point.

1993 as a not-for-profit organization dedicated to the health, safety and welfare of children. The Foundation, supported by both dealers and the Corporation, offers funding and marketing support to five national programs: Learn Not to Burn®, KIDestrians®, Stay Alert...Stay Safe®, Cycle Safe!® and AquaQuest™ — A Canadian Red Cross Water Safety Program. Canadian Tire also runs an environmental program in which thousands of tons of plastic, cardboard and paper are recycled. So are used oil and batteries from Canadian Tire Auto Centres. New stores are designed with energy-efficient lighting, heating and air-conditioning. In 1995 the company was awarded the Silver Award for Environmental Management by the *Financial Post*. But environmental awareness is just one of the ways Canadian Tire is positioning itself for the future. As Stephen Bachand put it in a recent State of the Tire address, "While we will hold true to the fundamental core values that still define the essence of Canadian Tire to generations of Canadians, we are literally remaking an enterprise here reshaping ourselves for tomorrow ... and doing it today."

For the Corporation's presidents over the years, for the Associate Dealers and for all their employees, change is never resisted, always embraced. At any point in its history, Canadian Tire's Associate Stores have never looked the same as they did five years before. Reinvention, improvement, adaptation, transformation are all integral to the store's success, and to its appeal to Canadians.

"I'd just love it if we still had a little store on Yonge Street," J.W. Billes once told Mayne Plowman. That desire for a simpler life is something we all can understand. But if J.W., and A.J., too, were alive today, they would take pride in seeing what the little store has become — a Canadian institution, a match for any American corporate behemoth, a chain of independently operated stores providing Canadians from coast to coast with good quality, affordable merchandise, and one of the finest retailers in the world fulfilling its vision "to be the best at what its customers value most."

Welcome to Dealerland

Far from home office in Toronto, in communities large and small from Belleville to Yarmouth, you'll find the network of Canadian Tire stores known collectively as "Dealerland." Out here you'll meet the entrepreneurial Associate Dealers who play such a key role in the company's success. Their dedication, their commitment to value and service and their community involvement make them the backbone of the company. This family album takes us on a nostalgic journey through Dealerland and shows how Canadian Tire has grown over the past seventy-five years.

Chateauguay, Quebec (left).

Charlottetown, Prince Edward Island, 1930s

Windsor, Nova Scotia, 1967

Calgary North, Alberta, 1987

118

Trois Rivières, Quebec, 1961

Yarmouth, Nova Scotia, 1969

Galt, Ontario, 1957

Hawkesbury, Ontario, 1979

Fenelon Falls, Ontario, 1947

Belleville, Ontario, 1940s

Estevan, Saskatchewan, 1978

Glace Bay, Nova Scotia, 1968

Valleyfield, Quebec, 1976

Toronto, Ontario, 1928 (left)

121

London North, Ontario, late 1980s

Corner Brook, Newfoundland, undated

Verdun, Quebec, 1968

Drummondville, Quebec, 1969

Trois Rivières, Quebec, 1961

Amherst, Nova Scotia, undated

Acknowledgments

A book covering 75 years of Canadian Tire history simply would not have been possible without the generous support and assistance provided by so many current and former Canadian Tire dealers and employees. In particular, I would like to thank Arch Brown, Sandy MacDonald, Dean Muncaster and Mayne Plowman for subjecting themselves to the interview process. I also wish to thank Myrel Pardoe, the gracious doyenne of Canadian Tire employees, for help, support and a prodigious memory spanning more than six decades of Canadian Tire history. Thanks, too, to Martha Billes and other members of the Billes family for so vigorously supporting the project and to Canadian Tire President Stephen Bachand for recognizing a good idea when he saw one.

— **Hugh McBride**

My thanks to Gord Sibley, for suggesting me for this job, and to Hugh Brewster and everyone at Madison Press Books and at Canadian Tire for giving me the creative leeway to develop the paintings you see in *Our Store*.

— **David Craig**

Madison Press Books would especially like to thank Roger Fox, president of the Canadian Tire Coupon Collectors Club, for granting us access to his extensive collection of Canadian Tire ephemera, and Jennifer Spaans and Jean Matheson, of the National Archives of Canada, for their incredible efforts in hunting down missing photographs under very tight deadlines. Thanks at Canadian Tire to Jennifer Garland and Aimee Norman-Leggat, for all their help in putting this project together.

Finally, Hugh McBride, Madison Press Books and Canadian Tire would all like to give a special thank you to Pat Stephenson, for her cheerful hospitality as Canadian Tire archivist and for her commitment to preserving the letters, records, catalogues and other material that have been left in her care.

Picture Credits

Page 33: (top and bottom left) City of Toronto Archives; (middle right) Private Collection (bottom right) TTC Archives

Page 34: (top left) Provincial Archives of Alberta; (bottom left) CBC Still Photo Collection

Page 36: (all) Collection of Roger Fox, photos by Laurie Coulter

Page 37: (top left) Reeves family; (top right) Provincial Archives of Nova Scotia

Page 38: (top and middle) Private Collection; (bottom) Reeves Family

Page 45: City of Vancouver Archives, photo by Claude Detloff

Page 46: (top) National Archives of Canada (C-29461); (inset) Saskatchewan Archives Board

Page 47: (top right) Provincial Archives of Manitoba; (bottom right) Provincial Archives of Alberta

Page 48: (top) Canadian War Museum; (bottom) Archives of Ontario

Page 49: (Left) National Archives of Canada (PA-114440); (top right) National Archives of Canada (C-108300); (bottom right) National Archives of Canada (PA-113486)

Page 52: (left) Private Collection

Page 59: (top left) Metro Toronto Archives; (middle left) Reeves Family

Page 62: (top left) National Archives of Canada (PA-116146); (top right) Provincial Archives of Alberta;

Page 63: (all) Collection of Roger Fox

Page 65: (bottom) The Hulton Getty Picture Collection Limited

Page 66: (top left) TTC Archives; (top right and bottom left) General Motors of Canada

Page 67: (top right) Provincial Archives of Manitoba

page 68: (bottom) Archives of Ontario

Page 69: (top right) Provincial Archives of Nova Scotia; (middle right) Archives of Ontario

Page 70: (left) Canadian Sports Hall of Fame; (top right) National Archives of Canada (C-20049); (bottom right) Archives of Ontario

Page 71: (left) Herb Nott for CBC; (right) Photo by John McNeill

Page 75: Roger Fox Collection

Page 76: (top) Governor General of Canada

Page 78: (top left) Provincial Archives of Alberta; (bottom right) Reeves Family

Page 79: (bottom left) Cruthers Family; (bottom right) Archives of Ontario

Page 81: (top right) Chrysler of Canada; (middle) Volkswagen

Page 83: (top and bottom left) CNE Archives Women's Division Fonds

Page 85: (all) Canada-Wide Feature Services

Page 89: (top) CNE Archives Women's Division Fonds

Page 94: (right) Photo by Frank Lennon/ The Toronto Star

Page 96: (top left) National Archives of Canada (C-27281); (middle left and right) The Toronto Star (right) Archives of Ontario

Page 97: (left) Photo by John McNeill

Page 108: (left) CANAPRESS; (right) Canadian Sports Hall of Fame

Page 109: (all) CANAPRESS

Index

Design, Typography and Art Direction:
Gordon Sibley Design

Editorial Director:
Hugh Brewster

Project Editors:
Laurie Coulter, Ian R. Coutts, Mireille Majoor

Editorial Assistance:
Susan Aihoshi

Production Director:
Susan Barrable

Production Coordinator:
Donna Chong

Colour Separations:
Colour Technologies

Printing and Binding:
Friesens Corporation

OUR STORE
was produced by Madison Press Books,
which is under the direction of
Albert E. Cummings